CW00522374

Dragonflies

of Bedfordshire

Stephen A Cham

The Bedfordshire Natural History Society

First published 2004
by The Bedfordshire Natural History Society

(Registered Charity No. 268659)

Apart from any fair dealing for the purposes of research or private study, or criticism or review, as permitted under the UK Copyright Designs and Patents Act, 1988, this publication may not be reproduced, stored, or transmitted, in any form or by any means, without the prior permission in writing of the publishers. Enquiries concerning reproduction outside the terms stated here should be sent to the publishers:

The Bedfordshire Natural History Society
c/o Bedford Museum
Castle Lane
Bedford MK40 3XD

British Library Cataloguing in Publication Data
A catalogue record for this book is available from the British Library.

ISBN 0 9506521 7 2

Credits
Maps - the Bedfordshire and UK boundaries used in the species distribution maps are based on Ordnance Survey maps.
Reproduced with kind permission of Ordnance Survey.
© Crown Copyright NC/04/44087

Text © 2004 Stephen Cham
Photographs © 2004 Stephen Cham

Typesetting and design by Stephen Cham

Printed and bound in Great Britain by Buckingham Colour, Buckingham
www.buckinghamcolour.com

Front cover photograph: Priory Country Park Finger Lakes and Broad-bodied Chaser.
Back cover photograph: Red-eyed Damselfly.
Title page photograph: Group of White-legged Damselflies ovipositing at Kempston Mill Backwater, July 1999.

Contents

Foreword

This is a must-have book for every naturalist in Bedfordshire. Indeed, even if you never set foot in the county, you will enjoy it and learn a great deal from it! It's a practical book for people who want to study dragonflies and do something to help them.

As leader of the Dragonfly Project, whose aim is to get the message across to people that dragonflies are beautiful, fascinating and in trouble, a book like this goes straight to my heart. Here, you will find basic details of dragonfly life-cycles and behaviour and simple recommendations for photographing dragonflies, for recording them and for assessing suitable habitats. It also includes detailed species descriptions of 21 of the dragonflies and damselflies you are most likely to find in Eastern England. The book is peppered with lively observations of dragonflies in action, from both Steve himself and his fellow Bedfordshire naturalists.

Much of what Steve has written is applicable to dragonflies throughout Britain. Indeed almost all of the information is directly transferable to Bedfordshire's neighbouring counties, who face identical challenges in terms of changes in land and water use.

On the desk beside me are seven other county dragonfly books and I hope the authors (some of whom are my friends!) of these very valuable works will not take offence if I say that in my view Steve's book sets a standard for others to follow.

It must have been at least fifteen years ago, at an Annual Indoor Meeting of the British Dragonfly Society, that Steve first impressed me. He and I were among the band of people asked to give talks during the day. While the rest of us lecturers fumbled about with handwritten transparencies on an asthmatic overhead projector, Steve's presentation was backed by two synchronised slide projectors with superb visuals. It wasn't simply his mastery of technology; it was the quality of the photographs; only those who had spent hours crawling about in undergrowth trying to get similar shots truly grasped the amount of effort which had gone into those beautiful slides. Steve also revealed a depth of knowledge about dragonflies you can only learn by spending years watching them on the wing.

Since then, Steve has worked tirelessly on behalf of dragonflies. His studies of the behaviour and habitat requirements of the Scarce Blue-tailed Damselfly (*Ischnura pumilio*) would alone have earned him a place in dragonfly history. You'll find his summary makes interesting reading. He has also shouldered the daunting task of setting up a national dragonfly recording scheme. This work is already bearing fruit, not just for dragonfly enthusiasts .... (wait till you see the distribution maps inside!) ... but it's also a fact that dragonflies are very good bio-indicators, so these records enable organisations such as Anglian Water and the Environment Agency to monitor the condition of countless sites.

Now, Steve has produced this outstanding book. And, typical Steve, it wears its erudition lightly. I'm sure you will enjoy it and find yourself turning to it again and again.

Ruary Mackenzie Dodds
Chairman of the Board of Trustees,
The Dragonfly Project
(formerly the National Dragonfly Biomuseum)

Preface

"About an hour later it (the Four-spotted Chaser) returned to its original position and remained there until 9.20pm. As it appeared to have gone to sleep at 9.20pm I decided to follow suit in my sleeping bag a few yards away. I woke up at 4.45 the following morning. In the dim light I could see the dragonfly. It had moved to another rush during the night. It had probably been disturbed by the cattle which had also spent the night in the field."

Norman Moore
(The Behaviour of the Adult Dragonfly[1])

Dragonflies have been a passion of mine for more than a quarter of a century. My interest was first kindled when I read the Collins New Naturalist book on Dragonflies, first published in 1966. The account of 'The Behaviour of the Adult Dragonfly' by Norman Moore left a lasting impression on me as a teenager. Norman describes how he wanted to study every aspect of their behaviour, which led him to spend a night in a field sleeping with them! I had to read on and as a result became totally hooked.

Dragonflies are a spectacular group of insects and they have inspired me to explore every corner of my home county (and beyond) in search of them. Norman's 'sleep-in' has motivated me on many occasions to get up before sunrise to go in search of dragonflies in the early morning light. At this time of day, before they become active, their bodies and wings are covered in dew and they rightfully stand out as the jewels in the landscape.

This book is more than just an account of dragonflies in Bedfordshire; it is as much about dragonfly habitats as it is the insects themselves. The protection and careful management of habitat ensures the continued survival of not just dragonflies but all wildlife in our countryside. Bedfordshire has seen many changes in its landscape over the years and this in turn has had an effect on dragonflies.

It provides guidance on where and how to observe dragonflies in Bedfordshire, which could be applicable to any other county in Great Britain. I have always had a special interest in studying dragonfly behaviour in order to understand what makes them 'tick'. There is still much that the amateur naturalist can contribute to the study of dragonflies in Britain. Many of the photographs and notes in this book refer to observations that may contribute to a better understanding of some of the fascinating behaviour they exhibit.

I hope that whatever their level of interest in dragonflies, readers will find something in this book that will make visits to the countryside more pleasurable. If the book helps to stimulate more interest and further study of Dragonflies in Bedfordshire and elsewhere, it will have served its purpose.

Steve Cham (Silsoe 2003)

▶ Four-spotted Chaser at dawn. The wings and body are covered with tiny beads of dew. Note how the darker parts of the body and wings are warmer and so repel the dew. This photograph was taken just after sunrise at 6.00am, July 2000.

Reference
[1] Corbet,P.S., Longfield,C. & Moore,N.W. (1960)

Introduction

Dragonflies are among the most beautiful and spectacular insects flying today. They are often very distinctive and can usually be seen wherever there is clean freshwater. They are also one of the most ancient groups of insect. The group has the scientific name Odonata and is one of the smaller of the thirty or so insect Orders. The Order Odonata is equivalent to beetles (Coleoptera), or flies (Diptera), or butterflies and moths (Lepidoptera), and so on. British Dragonflies fall into two distinct sub-orders, the damselflies and the true-dragonflies. To avoid confusion, in this book Dragonfly written with a capital 'D' means the entire Order, i.e. the Odonata, and dragonfly with a lower case 'd' means the sub-order 'true-dragonflies'.

Worldwide, 5000+ species of Dragonfly have been described, with the highest numbers of species living in the tropics, mainly in rainforest. They are relatively primitive insects. They first appeared in the Carboniferous period, 300 million years ago. In France huge fossil dragonflies with a wingspan of 700mm have been found, over five times the size of the largest dragonfly living today. About 50 species have been recorded from the British Isles.

As mentioned above, the Dragonflies form the Order Odonata; this scientific name refers to the tooth-like ridges on the mandibles. The two sub-orders into which the British species are subdivided are:

Zygoptera meaning "similar wings", these are the damselflies and are recognisable by the rather similar shape of their forewing and hindwing and by the way they fold their wings together along the body when at rest.

Anisoptera meaning "unequal wings", these are the true-dragonflies and are recognisable by the way they rest with wings outstretched, at right angles to the body, and by the different shape of their forewing and hindwing.

Dragonflies are predators at each stage of their life cycle. They form an important component of wetland wildlife and play a significant role in its ecology. The abundance of Dragonfly larvae reflects the well-being of the aquatic life on which they feed. Since most species of Dragonfly are unable to tolerate even mildly polluted water, they have potential as indicators of the health of an aquatic environment. As adults they have a particular advantage in that their conspicuous colours and behaviour enable numbers to be

◄ Damselfly and dragonfly larvae are voracious predators. This is an often overlooked stage of their life cycle, which plays a significant role in their natural history. Some species such as the Azure Damselfly (right) spend much of their time hunting for prey in underwater plants, whereas the well concealed Broad-bodied Chaser lies in wait for its prey.

counted relatively quickly and easily. This provides a cost effective means of measuring the health or sickness of the habitat[1]. As an example, the number of species present on a lake or stretch of river can be compared with the number at a similar but unpolluted site. Over longer timescales, regular monitoring at sites and county surveys provide means for detecting changes in aquatic environments. A large section of this book is dedicated to dragonfly habitats and their conservation. Without this we would not have the wealth of species that breed in the county.

Identification and biology

It is not intended that this book should be a comprehensive guide to the identification of Bedfordshire dragonflies nor to provide detailed information on the biology of each species. There are many excellent publications that cover these subjects in detail. For identification in the field one of the up-to-date field guides[2] should be consulted. For those seeking a full account of dragonfly natural history and biology there is no better text than Corbet[3], which provides a wealth of information.

The text for each species is intended to give readers some background information on what they may encounter in the county with pointers as to what to look for in the field. Notes of caution are also given where the possibilities of misidentification or confusion with other species is possible. It is recommended that a field guide be consulted in all cases of uncertainty. Where rare species are recorded, a colour photograph or voucher specimen may be required before the record can be accepted by the Dragonfly Recording Network. Where appropriate, details of characteristic behaviour are given as an aid to distinguishing species. For some species, extracts from the author's field notes have been included to describe behaviour and other points of interest.

For those readers new to entomology (the study of insects) it is sometimes possible to get confused or even put off by the extensive use of scientific names. These are usually derived from Latin or Greek and even naturalists, who find them difficult to remember, often avoid them. There are compelling reasons to try to learn them. The use of scientific names and the classification of living organisms were introduced to avoid the confusion that can develop when different people use local anecdotal or vernacular names. A species that has the prefix of 'common' may be common in one area but local or rare in others. The Common Hawker for example is absent from Bedfordshire and has declined in Britain to the point at which it is now probably less widespread than the Southern, Brown and Migrant Hawkers. In fact, the Migrant Hawker formerly known as the Scarce Hawker, is now more 'common' than the Common Hawker in most of England. The Norfolk Hawker *Aeshna isosceles* is a rare, Red Data species confined to Norfolk and Suffolk, yet widespread in many parts of the Mediterranean. Such use of 'English' names can only serve to add confusion especially when travelling abroad. One should try to learn scientific names. *Pyrrhosoma nymphula* translated as 'flame-bodied water nymph' has a somewhat more aesthetic appeal than Large Red Damselfly.

Acknowledgements

The publication of this book would not have been possible without the input and assistance of a great number of people. Members of the Bedfordshire Natural History Society have been especially instrumental in contributing to the Dragonfly Recording Network over many years. I would like to extend a special thankyou to Dr Nancy Dawson who preceded me as county recorder for greatly assisting in the transfer of county records and providing me with relevant information from her field notes. The Scientific Commitee and Council of the Bedfordshire Natural History Society have given support in many ways.

I am grateful to Charles Baker for bringing my attention to the historical records contained in the Revd. C. Abbot's "*Lepidoptera Anglica cum Libellulis*" and the dragonfly records in J.C.Dale's collection. I would also like to thank Dr Bernard Verdcourt, Dr Derek Reid and Mr Bernard West for providing me details of their past records for Bedfordshire. Brian Eversham kindly brought my attention to the communications relating to the records of Scarce Emerald Damselfly and Christine Shepperson has shared records and notes from Hertfordshire. Andy McGeeney and Dave Winsland have provided useful advice on dragonfly behaviour and recording over the years. Gill Hendley of English Heritage has kindly allowed me access to Wrest Park to monitor the dragonflies. Dave Ball for sharing his field notes relating to the discovery of Small Red-eyed Damselfly.

All Bedfordshire dragonfly records have been computerised using BioBase recording software developed by Mike Thurner. Mike helped with software issues during the initial stages of computerising the Bedfordshire records. The distribution maps were prepared using Mike Thurner's SmartMap to transfer data from BioBase to Alan Morton's DMAP mapping software. Thank you to Paul Harding and Henry Arnold for making available historical records formerly held at the Biological Records Centre at Monks Wood. I would like to thank Charles Baker, Chris Boon, Rosemary Brind, Dr Bernard Nau and Mary Sheridan for constructive comments on the draft manuscript and to Phil Cannings for his advice in the preparation work. To my three sons Mark, Phillip and James for their skills at finding things odonate; these are usually closer to the ground, higher in the air or in more awkward places than adults often look. Last but not least to my wife Lesley for support over the years.

Finally to those who have submitted records or information:

J.Adams, J.M.Adams, A.Aldhous, D.M.Allen, P.Almond, B.Anderson, D.Anderson, K.Anderson, H.Arnold, V.W.Arnold, D.Ashwell, C.R.B.&P.M.Baker, D.Ball, K.Balmer, C.Banks, A.&M.Banthorpe, M.Bates, G.Bellamy, P.Bennett, S.Blain, P.Bird, C.R.Boon, R.Bradshaw, T.Bratton, R.Brind, S.Brooke, S.J.Brooks, A.Brownett, A.Bucknall, C.W.Burton, P.Cannings, L.Carman, C.Carpenter, Dr Challoners, J.C.Cham, L.A.Cham, M.A.Cham, P.A.Cham, S.A.Cham, V.H.Chambers, W.J.Champkin, A.Chapman, T.D.Charlton, J.Childs, P.Clarke, J.Comont, A.Copeland, A.Dassington, I.K.Dawson, N.Dawson, J.Day, R.Dazley, D.Dell, J.Dempster, G.Dennis, A&G.Dickens, A.Dickson, J.Dixon, A.Donelly, A.Doody, J.Dony, W.J.Drayton, C.Eddleston, P.Escott, B.Eversham, M.Fail, R.Fail, A.Fleckney, T.Gladwin, P.Glenister, D.Green, J.M.Green, M.Greenall, J.Halls, B.D.Harding, P.Harding, G.Hendley, B.Hook, C.Horton, P.Howard, J.Howe, A.Hurst, P.Hyman, B.M.Inns, P.Irving, M.Izzard, T.James, H.Jones, M.Kemp, J.Kemp-Gee, H.A.S.Key, D.Lawrence, R.Lawrence, W.J.LeQuesne, K.Lewis, P.Knight, C.Longfield, A.J.Martin, P.Madgett, J.Mason, Br.J.Mayhead, R.Merritt, M.McCarrick, N.Miller, N.Milton, H.Minter, H.Muir-Howie, B.Nau, A.Nelson, E.Newman, B.Nightingale, M.O'Brien, P.Oldfield, D.A.Orwin, G.Osborne, A.R.Outen, R.Pallister, M.Palmer, R.A.Palmer, A.Paynter D.Parsons, V.Perrin, A.Peterkin, M.Peterkin, N.J.Phillips, G.Pilkington, S.Pittman, S.Plummer, M.Powell, I.Procter, A.Proud, D.Rands, E.B.Rands, S.Raven, D.A.Reid, N.Renwick, R.C.Revels, A.Reynolds, P.J.Rhodes, J.Rowe, M.B.Rowland, T.Sanderson, V.Scott, M.W.Service, K.Sharpe, J.T.R.Sharrock, C.Shepperson, M.Sheridan, G.Sherwin, M.Skelton, M.Smout, A.Smith, P.Smith, B.R.Squires, C.Tack, T.Thomas, A.S.Tifley, P.Trodd, T.J.Thomas, D.Tyler, B.Verdcourt, M.Watson, C.Watts, K.Webb, K.Weedon, M.Weedon, B.B.West, D.Wickings, M.Williams, S.G.Williams, T.Williams, D.Wilson, K.Winder, D.Winsland, H.Winter, D.T.Withers, I.Woiwood, N.Wood, R.Woolnough

References

[1] Moore (1997)

[2] Brooks (1997, 2002)

[3] Corbet (1999)

Dragonfly body form - a brief overview

Dragonflies have the same basic body plan as all other insects, such as Beetles and Butterflies. Their bodies are divided into three main parts; head, thorax and abdomen. For Dragonflies this plan is similar in both the larval and adult stages. It is important to have an understanding of insect anatomy as it not only plays a vital role in their biology but is also essential for the identification of species.

The shape, size and ratio between various body parts needs to be measured in order to identify certain larvae. Fortunately, this can be done with live specimens without any harm coming

▶ Damselfly larva

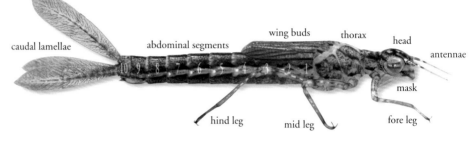

▶ Dragonfly larva

NB. The larval wing buds project back as far as the fourth abdominal segment. This is characteristic of a final instar larvae.

Emergence - the transformation of larva............

2.11 am

The dragonfly larva emerges from the water, climbing a suitable perch to gain a firm foothold. The larval skin splits along the dorsal surface allowing the head and thorax to slowly push free.

2.27 am

After the head, thorax and legs are free the emerging adult enters the resting phase. This enables the legs to harden before it pulls itself completely free of the larval skin.

2.45 am

The newly emerged adult dragonfly is now free of the larval skin, which is now referred to as the exuvia. This can be collected after the adult has flown.

2.50 am

The dragonfly pumps fluid into the wing membranes which start to expand quite rapidly. At the same time the abdomen grows in length.

to them. Most larvae can be readily identified to species with or without the use of suitable published keys [1,2,3].

The identification of adults may require an assessment of the distribution of colour on the abdominal segments or thorax. Colour of abdominal segments is often a quick way to separate species. For example the males of Blue-tailed and Scarce Blue-tailed Damselflies are distinguished by the amount of blue on segments 8, 9 and 10 (see photographs for numbering).

The sex of adult dragonflies can be determined by looking for the presence of an ovipositor in the females. The precursor for this can also be seen on larvae. In adult males the secondary genitalia can be seen on the underside of abdominal segment 2. The shape and size of the anal appendages is also diagnostic.

◀ Compound eye of a Common Darter. The individual 'cells' or ommatidia are larger at the top of the eye, getting smaller towards the bottom. This differentiation enables the eye to detect both movement as well as detail.

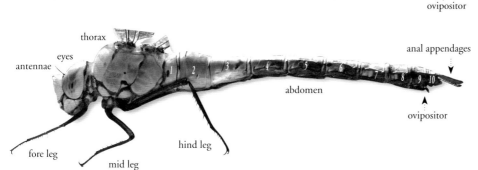

thorax
antennae
eyes
fore leg
mid leg
hind leg
abdomen
ovipositor

◀ Damselfly - adult female. NB. the wings are not shown.

thorax
eyes
antennae
fore leg
mid leg
hind leg
abdomen
anal appendages
ovipositor

◀ Dragonfly - adult female. NB. The wings are not shown.

References
[1] Miller (1995)
[2] Brooks (2002)
[3] Smallshire and Swash (2004)
(see glossary for additional information.)

.... to adult

3.05 am

The wings and abdomen have nearly reached their full length. They have a milky white colour at this stage.

3.25 am

The wings start to harden and slowly clear. The abdomen attains its full size.

4.30 am

The wings open and the adult dragonfly will 'sit it out' until the sun rises.

◀ The emergence of a large conspicuous dragonfly, such as this Southern Hawker, typically takes place at night in order to avoid predation. This sequence was photographed in the early hours of the morning from a fixed camera position.

Watching dragonflies in Bedfordshire

Bedfordshire is one of the smallest English counties, spanning some 60 kilometres north to south and 40 kilometres east to west. It has a varied landscape and prominent landmarks that reflect the underlying geology. This in turn determines the occurrence of wetland habitats that attract dragonflies. Twelve species of damselfly and sixteen species of dragonfly have been recorded in Bedfordshire either as resident species or casual migrants. Currently ten species of damselfly and eleven species of dragonfly breed in the county.

When and where

It is not generally realised that the adult dragonflies, seen flying around during the summer months, constitute just a short part of their total life cycle. Dragonflies overwinter either as eggs or larvae, with the major part of the life cycle spent underwater as larvae. Larval development can take up to five years in Britain depending on latitude and local microhabitat conditions. In Bedfordshire all species complete their life cycle in 1 to 2 years. The larvae of most species can be found either partially concealed in mud and silt at the bottom of a pond or river or climbing through underwater vegetation in search of prey. Larvae pass through a series of instars before they are ready to transform into the adult dragonfly. The emergence process typically takes place during the hours of darkness or early morning in order to avoid predation. Once leaving the water the process can take several hours. The newly emerged adult dragonfly will typically direct its maiden flight away from water, flying into surrounding meadows and woodland. Newly emerged or teneral adults fly away from water to undergo maturation and to avoid the unwanted attentions of territorial adult males at the breeding site. Prevailing weather conditions influence the emergence period and cool wet periods will delay emergence. During the first week after emergence adults become sexually mature and attain their brilliant colours. Care should be taken with identification of immature forms as their colours can differ from older specimens (as well as those in some field guides).

Adult Dragonflies are on the wing for a relatively short period (approximately six weeks) during the warmer months of the year and all Bedfordshire species can be seen between the months of May and September. In favourable years with a warm spring the first species to appear is the Large Red Damselfly which starts to emerge during April. At the other end of the season Common Darter and Migrant Hawker can be still seen flying in late-November, exceptionally into December.

Dragonflies can be observed under suitable weather conditions at almost any non-polluted wetland in the county. They are sun-loving insects and are best searched for on warm, sunny days with little or no wind. Areas sheltered from strong winds are likely to be more

Flight periods:

Flight periods for each species are given in the flight period charts (p16-19). First and last dates are given in the individual species accounts.

▼ White-legged Damselfly covered with early morning dew at Kempston Mill. Note how the front pair of legs is being used like a comb to remove the beads of dew from around the eyes and antennae.

productive than exposed ones. Their large size and bright colours quickly catch the eye of the observer and a few minutes spent carefully watching can reveal a fascinating array of behaviour. The males of the larger species can be seen by water, tirelessly flying back and forth in search of females. The common names of dragonflies such as Hawker, Chaser, Darter and Skimmer reflect the behavioural traits and flight patterns of each species. Dragonflies are often seen flying along woodland rides in search of insect prey. Woodland, even some distance from water, can provide ideal feeding habitat.

The smaller damselflies are most often encountered at the breeding site and in surrounding meadows where they can often be seen in high numbers. The larger dragonflies are more territorial and vigorously defend territories at the breeding sites. For this reason fewer individuals will be encountered. If one wishes to observe dragonfly behaviour, then the breeding sites should be sought out, as it is here that most activity will occur. Female dragonflies spend less time at water in order to avoid male competition, returning to mate and oviposit.

During cold, overcast conditions

adults become lethargic and will shelter in vegetation. They are best searched for low down in thick vegetation close to the waterside. They will also use such sites to roost overnight. Early morning visits to suitable sites will often reveal many individuals perched in a small area.

The weather can be highly variable during the summer months. To remain active dragonflies need to maintain their body temperature within certain limits. In the early morning when air temperatures are cool they need to raise their body temperature to prepare for the first flight of the day. They will orientate their bodies to catch the maximum strength from the rising sun. Vegetation and roosting dragonflies become covered in dew during cool early morning conditions. Dragonflies will use their forelegs to clean away droplets of water from the eyes and other sensory organs. On exceptionally warm days one can observe the opposite effect when they need to cool their body temperature down. They point their abdomen towards the sun to reduce the amount of body surface area exposed to direct heating.

A number of species are on the edge of their range in Britain. For example the Scarce Blue-tailed Damselfly, which can be found in Bedfordshire, is a stenotopic[1] species confined to a narrow range of habitat requirements. Water temperature is one of the limiting factors for its site selection. The shallow seepage habitat where it occurs warms quickly, thus creating conditions for rapid larval development. These spring fed seepages remain frost and ice free even in relatively cold winters and this again enables the species to survive.

▲ Ruddy Darter adopting the 'obelisk' posture to reduce the amount of body area exposed to the sun. Record summer temperatures were experienced during August 2003 when this photograph was taken at Milton Bryan.

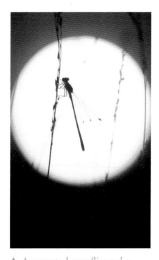

▲ At sunset, dragonflies seek a suitable place to roost. Here a Common Blue Damselfly sits out the night on a grass stem.

◀ Banded Demoiselle roosting overnight in dense bankside vegetation by the River Great Ouse at Turvey.

◀ In late summer Common Darters bask on light coloured surfaces to absorb the reflected warmth.

Predators, parasites and prey

Dragonflies play an important role in the ecology of other organisms. They are preyed upon by a number of species of bird and amphibians as well as spiders and other invertebrates. In turn they prey upon many invertebrates, especially other insects. Observations of predation on dragonflies in Bedfordshire can contribute to a greater understanding of their natural history.

Birds

Birds are probably the most frequently observed predator of dragonflies in Bedfordshire. There have been numerous reports of Hobbies and other birds of prey catching dragonflies in the county. Hobbies have regularly been seen catching dragonflies at Sundon Chalk Quarry [2] and in the Marston Vale Clay Pits. During June 2002 at Halls Pit, Blunham, the author observed a Hobby at close range taking Emperor dragonflies as they hawked around the lake. They typically fly low over water to capture the dragonfly, then as they fly up they hold their prey in one talon whilst the inedible wings are bitten off. It is an unforgettable experience to watch this behaviour and to see the discarded wings slowly float to the ground as the prey is eaten. A Kestrel was observed taking Migrant Hawkers along the margins of Kings Wood, Houghton Conquest in 1991. It has been suggested that the increased abundance of Common Darter and Migrant Hawker during August and September has contributed to the increasing post fledgling survival of Hobbies [3].

On several occasions, piles of dragonfly wings, especially those of Banded Demoiselle have been discovered on the banks of the River Great Ouse. At first it is not always obvious what is responsible for these, unless you sit and watch. Pied and Grey Wagtails have been observed taking Banded Demoiselles along stretches of the river at Felmersham, Harrold and Kempston. At Kempston Church End on 4th July 1993 a pair of Pied Wagtails was observed repeatedly flying over the river to take adult male Banded Demoiselles. Each time they returned to the same spot, before biting off the wings and consuming their prey. A small pile of the Demoiselle wings was found on the river bank.

Insects

Insects are both predators and prey of dragonflies. Tony Smith observed a Brown Hawker catch and eat a Small White Butterfly at Radwell. He also observed a Southern Hawker catch a small damselfly, then flying into a tree to consume it. Joan Childs reported a Brown Hawker catch and consume a Large White Butterfly at Felmersham. A similar observation was made by Nancy Dawson in 1978 where one was observed biting off the wings of the butterfly before consuming the rest. The author observed a female Hairy Dragonfly break off from ovipositing to catch a male Azure Damselfly and consume it on a nearby bush at Priory Park. The author also observed a patrolling male Emperor feeding on late emerging Banded Demoiselles at Kempston Mill in June 2003.

▼ "A female Brown Hawker was observed ovipositing into exposed roots at the margins of one of the ponds at Marston Thrift. She stopped egg laying and flew up from the water to catch a male Common Darter, which had been flying out from a nearby perch. This was large prey for a Brown Hawker and a struggle ensued before it could gain a firm hold. I moved around the bank to get a closer look but disturbed the female, which flew off. I found the Common Darter and to my surprise most of the abdomen had already been eaten, with only its thorax and head still intact. Despite this it was still alive and firmly gripping a twig. I stayed with it until it finally showed no further signs of life, one and a half hours later."

(Extract from author's field notes – 5th August 1998)

Palmer[4] recalls finding an adult Common Darter at Flitwick Moor that had been caught by the larva of the Green Tiger Beetle *Cicindela campestris*. The dragonfly was held to the ground in a helpless condition as the beetle larva dragged one of the hind wings down into its burrow. This behaviour is known to occur where there are large colonies of this carnivorous beetle[5] and indicates what the habitat conditions at Flitwick Moor might have been like at the time.

Hornets are active hunters and will attack dragonflies if they get the chance. They have been observed catching dragonflies as large as Southern and Migrant Hawkers. If the prey is too large for them to tackle in one go they will dismember parts of the body so they can take it back to their nest in more manageable amounts. The author observed a Hornet kill and butcher a Migrant Hawker at Felmersham NR. The Hornet made several trips to take body parts back to its nest.

Barry Nightingale observed a Hornet attack a Southern Hawker in his back garden:

"*On 28th August 1995 I watched a Hornet catch a Southern Hawker (it mounted it from the top) and the two came down onto the lawn. The dragonfly was not dead and as I felt sorry for it I 'rescued' it and removed it about 10 yards away into a flower border. The most remarkable thing was that the Hornet returned to the area of lawn where it had brought down the dragonfly and covered the area by flying like a harrier up and down. It did not re-find the dragonfly which subsequently died.*"

On the 9th September 2003 at Felmersham NR the author witnessed a male Ruddy Darter fall onto the water surface. The unfortunate dragonfly had been attempting to mate with a female when the pair fell on the water. The female managed to get free and fly away but the male quickly became waterlogged. The vibration of the wings quickly attracted Pond Skaters *Gerris* sp. as well as a few Water Crickets *Velia caprai*. When the dragonfly had stopped struggling the bugs moved in until the dragonfly's body was covered by over twenty, each trying to feed on the body.

▲ A male Ruddy Darter is quickly overcome by Pond Skaters (*Gerris* sp) and Water Crickets (*Velia caprai*). They feed by probing the soft parts between the body segments. Felmersham NR September 2003.

Spiders

As predators of dragonflies, spiders can be subdivided into those that use webs to catch their prey and those that actively hunt them. To the author's knowledge there are no observations of hunting spiders taking dragonflies in the county. Bedfordshire lacks the habitat for the larger hunting spiders such as the Raft Spider *Dolomedes*

◄ Hornet attacking a Migrant Hawker at Felmersham NR September 2003. After paralysing it with its sting the Hornet butchered the dragonfly by removing the head and thorax, before flying off to its nest. A Muscid Fly landed on the remains to feed before the Hornet returned to carry off the abdomen.

▲ A Blue-tailed Damselfly caught in the web of the spider *Tetragnatha extensa* at Coronation Pit. A male Scorpion Fly *Panorpa communis* can be seen 'raiding' the web to feed on the entangled damselfly.

fimbriatus.

In contrast, there are many observations of web spinning spiders catching various dragonfly species. A casual walk along the River Great Ouse will often reveal Banded Demoiselles entrapped in the webs of different spiders.

Some dragonfly species appear to actively avoid spider webs. The larger Hawker species can sometimes free themselves using their body mass. Dragonflies are occasionally observed with remnants of web silk on their wings resulting from a lucky escape.

Fish

Predation of adult dragonflies by fish is a rarely reported occurrence. During August 2003 at one of the ponds in Wrest Park small Rudd were observed approaching and trying to catch egg laying tandems of Red-eyed Damselfly and Small Red-eyed Damselfly. Most attempts resulted in the damselflies detecting the fish below the surface and flying off to a new site. However, on several occasions the fish were seen with the abdomen of female damselflies projecting from their mouth. In one such case a fish grabbed and bit off the abdomen of an ovipositing female leaving the thorax, head and wings still alive on the water's surface. Several males attempted to retrieve this female

without success.

Amphibians

Common Frog *Rana temporaria* is the amphibian most often observed catching dragonflies. They sit in wait and leap out at adults when they detect movement. At garden ponds, frogs have been observed leaping at ovipositing females of Common Darter and Broad-bodied Chaser. The author's personal observations suggest that the success rate of these attacks is very low.

Newts, especially Smooth Newts *Triturus vulgaris* will take dragonfly larvae. Smooth Newts were seen to feed on damselfly larvae by systematically searching amongst aquatic plants at the author's garden pond.

Mammals

The most widely reported mammalian predator of dragonflies is the Domestic Cat. They are attracted to the movement and noise of the wings and will readily try to catch them. Southern Hawkers are played with whilst still alive in much the same way as with mice. During 2001 a part eaten Southern Hawker was found in one of the Dormouse release cages at Maulden Wood[6]. The dragonfly had been caught during night time foraging and taken back to be eaten. The dragonfly had most of its thorax eaten away, which would have provided a nutritious meal.

Mites

Many dragonfly and damselfly species carry parasitic mites. The mites attach themselves by probing their mouthparts between the segments and soft parts of the body. Infestation load tends to vary each year. In Bedfordshire mites have been reported on Azure, Common Blue and Blue-tailed Damselflies. In some years the high numbers of Red-eyed and Small Red-eyed Damselflies at Wrest Park can result in a high burden of mites. Some individuals have been seen with the entire length of the ventral surface of the abdomen covered with them.

Estimating numbers

Watching Dragonflies and recording observations can contribute to a better understanding of even our common species. Dragonfly records have greater value if some estimation of numbers of each life stage is made. There are several ways in which this can be done and one should be aware of the advantages and limitations of each method.

1. Counting
2. Transect walks
3. Capture-mark-recapture

Counting

Adult Dragonflies are highly mobile and provide a challenge to count. There are many factors that will influence the numbers of flying adults at any given time. For the best results, survey work should be carried out under near optimal weather conditions for activity. Ideally visits should be made when it is warm and sunny, little cloud cover and preferably with little wind (less than Force 3 or 4 on the Beaufort scale). Most species, once they have emerged, disperse into surrounding areas and therefore the best time to count adults is at emergence. This in itself can be problematic, as it requires timing the visit when adults are emerging. Simply counting adults does <u>not</u> provide a reliable estimate of the population size at a site. In addition to the factors discussed above, the numbers counted can vary between recorders. The experience of the person doing the count and the amount of time spent will produce different results.

The national Dragonfly Recording Network has used a system for estimating the numbers of the different life stages of dragonflies when working in the field that enables trends to be analysed. This system has been used for many years to estimate various dragonfly life stages and is used as the basis of the species maps showing adult abundance. The RA70 recording card enables these estimates of numbers to be noted when recording.

A	1 only
B	2-5
C	6-20
D	21-100
E	100-500
F	500+

The life stages recorded are:

Adults – adult only sightings (can be away from the breeding site)

Copulating pairs – males and females in the process of mating (can be away from the breeding site)

Ovipositing females – females or tandem pairs in the process of laying eggs (whilst this will take place at water it is not proof that the eggs or larvae will be able to develop to adulthood)

Larvae – recording larvae is a means of proving that a species is breeding. Strictly such records should be made on final instar larvae indicating that larval development can be completed.

Exuviae – The larval skin that is cast during the transformation process to an adult dragonfly proves that a species can complete its life cycle.

Emergents (pre-flight) – Dragonflies observed in the process of emergence from larvae to adult. Newly emerged dragonflies are called tenerals. During this phase the wings of the emerging dragonfly appear shiny and the body has not attained its full colouration. Care should be taken to determine the breeding site once they are able to fly, especially when different habitats, such as running and stillwater, are immediately adjacent to each other.

Regular collecting of exuviae will reveal how many individuals have emerged from a breeding site. An exuvia is an exact replica of the final instar larvae and most can be readily identified and sexed with a 10X-hand lens. This not only provides one of the most reliable ways of assessing total numbers but also if collected regularly demonstrates the length of the emergence period. By collecting exuviae it often comes as a surprise to find out how many individuals have emerged. In excess of one hundred dragonflies have been reported emerging from small garden ponds no more than a few metres square.

Pond 'dipping' for dragonfly larvae with a suitable net is one of the best ways to obtain proof of breeding for a given species. The best times to find larvae will depend on the target species. Springtime is usually best as during the winter period larvae move into deeper water and can be especially difficult to locate. Various designs of net are available from specialist suppliers, yet fixing a kitchen strainer to the end of a broom handle can make a simple and effective net. The study of larvae, especially their feeding behaviour can be a rewarding pastime. Most larvae can be kept in a small aquarium indoors and should be fed every few days. Depending on their size, food should be varied: *Daphnia* for small larvae, bloodworms for medium sized species, and earthworms for large dragonfly larvae.

With little or no experience it is possible to make useful contributions to our knowledge and understanding. Dragonflies visiting or emerging from garden and school ponds provide useful information about local species. Those

with garden ponds may occasionally see single male or female Southern Hawker visiting for short periods. Collections of exuviae made at a school or village pond can provide a worthwhile project in which to involve children.

Transect Walks

A transect walk provides a more standardised means of recording dragonfly numbers over a period of time. It requires a defined route to be walked at regular intervals during the flight season and under optimal weather conditions (as discussed above). This method was first developed by Norman Moore at Monks Wood Experimental Station to monitor dragonfly numbers[7]. It was later adopted by Ernie Pollard for the Butterfly Monitoring Scheme and became known as the Pollard walk. It is still a very popular means of estimating butterfly numbers.

Transect walks require a considerable commitment in time. The method looks at trends rather than absolute numbers and in the case of dragonflies tends to give an underestimate of population size. Some dragonfly monitoring has been carried out in the county but it has been intermittent as it relies so heavily on a few individuals.

Capture-mark-recapture

Counting the numbers of adult Dragonflies, either casually or as part of a transect walk, is likely to give an underestimate of numbers when compared to the capture-mark-recapture method. In some cases this can vary by up to a factor of ten[8]. The method involves catching adult Dragonflies

Keeping larvae: A caution! [10]

Care should be taken when collecting larvae for observation at home. Larvae kept in an indoor aquarium develop rapidly if well fed. They can emerge prematurely, whilst outdoor temperatures are too cold for adults to survive. The best time to overcome this problem is to collect during the spring and early summer so that larvae can be observed before they emerge. Adults can then be released into favourable weather conditions. Wherever possible, adults and larvae should be released from the site where they were collected. Unavoidable release of adult dragonflies away from their normal distribution should be reported to the local recorder.

▶ Members of the Bedfordshire Natural History Society 'pond dipping' at Priory Country Park Finger Lakes. A large plastic sheet is ideal for sorting and then releasing the catch back into the water.

and marking their wings with a unique identifier. Upon release the dragonflies are monitored over a period of time either by recapturing them or by direct observation. The latter is possible if the marking can be seen clearly either at rest or in flight. By recording the numbers of marked individuals that are recaptured or seen, one can get a better estimate of the population size. However, to carry out this technique requires an even greater commitment of time throughout the season and for this reason it is usually left to professional biologists.

The discovery of Scarce Blue-tailed Damselfly at Sundon and Houghton Regis chalk quarries raised a number of questions. Not only were the sites many hundred kilometres from the nearest known colonies but they were also regarded as highly atypical. A more detailed study of the habitat requirements for this species therefore seemed appropriate. As the study developed, it became apparent that the various colour forms of the females were not present in equal numbers throughout the flight season. In addition, the males appeared to have greatly differing success at mating with the different colour forms. Capture-mark-recapture therefore seemed appropriate to carry out further study into the development and behaviour of this species. During the summer of 1992, 628 adults were marked at Sundon Chalk Quarry[8]. The wings were clearly marked with a numbering system using a fine indelible ink marker pen. This did not harm the damselflies in any way and did not affect their behaviour in an adverse way (see photo above). Marked individuals were monitored regularly during the flight season between May and September and detailed records made of sexual activity and interactions between individuals. Notes were also made of any colour changes that occurred during maturation. The study found that there were many more individuals at the site than counting on a transect

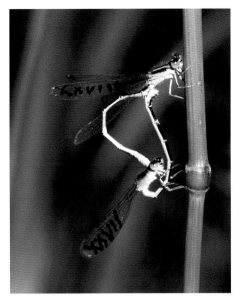

walk. It was also possible to show for the first time that females did not have distinct forms as previously thought and underwent age related colour changes. The bright orange *aurantiaca* female is a transitional colour phase and develops into the green-brown colouration of the fully mature female. Such findings would not have been possible without marking individuals. The study also concluded that whilst the habitat conditions of the base rich seepages at Sundon appeared at first glance to be very different to the traditional acid bog habitats, they were in fact very similar physically at a microhabitat level[9].

◀ Scarce Blue-tailed Damselflies 'in-cop', shortly after being marked for a capture-mark-recapture study at Sundon in 1992. This photograph clearly demonstrates, that if carefully done, the marking does not affect their natural behaviour.

▼ A variation of the mark-recapture method used to monitor return visits of Southern Hawkers to the author's garden pond in Silsoe (see species section on Southern Hawker). One can approach very closely to apply the markings (see appendix 2). The photograph shows the 4-red dot female on one of her return visits to oviposit in an old log during September 2003.

▲ When trying the close approach some species, such as this Emerald Damselfly, will move around a stem to avoid detection. (Milton Bryan, July 2003)

Getting closer

For the casual dragonfly watcher, the naked eye can be adequate for observing the most easily recognised species. As one's interest develops more detailed observations will require some form of magnifying device.

Binoculars are the most readily available optics and have widespread use amongst naturalists. Careful consideration should be given to the closest focussing distance, which will be necessary for close viewing of damselflies. Whilst high magnification may seem desirable it can induce shake that will make viewing difficult. In recent years several models with image stabilisation have become available but often at the detriment of close focussing. Dragonflies will most often be observed close to water where looking into the light and reflections will test the quality of anti-reflective lens coating. Binoculars should ideally be tested before purchase, preferably on a sunny day when the degree of flare can be assessed. Gas filled waterproof binoculars are also worth considering especially when working near to water.

Monoculars offer an alternative viewing system, especially when working at close range. They usually allow very close focussing, sometimes less than one metre. A range of magnifications is available and the final choice depends on an individual's ability to handhold the optic for steady viewing. When approaching close, care should be taken to avoid casting a shadow on the subject.

Telescopes offer additional magnifying power, especially when insects are observed from a distance. They need to be used on a tripod, which adds an additional burden for carrying. The discovery of the Small Red-eyed Damselfly in Bedfordshire was the result of careful searching through a telescope (Dave Ball's discovery is recalled under the account for this species).

Catching Dragonflies

If adult dragonflies need to be caught for further examination a round framed or kite net with a soft mesh should be used. A purposeful stroke from behind the insect should be used with a quick flick of the wrist to seal the net. A stroke from the front should be avoided as it can damage the tactile hairs and sensory organs on the head of the dragonfly. In Britain the Norfolk Hawker *Aeshna isosceles* is protected by law and a licence is required if it to be netted or handled.

It should be re-emphasised that dragonfly sites need to be assessed by the number of breeding species they support. Whilst a species list is useful in determining the species present, it does not provide a true reflection of the ability of the habitat to support a sustained population. Individuals wandering from nearby sites may not find all sites suitable for breeding. Recording proof of breeding and estimates of numbers present provides much better data on which to base habitat management plans.

Collecting Dragonflies: A caution! [10]

The taking of live adult or larval dragonflies for collections is to be discouraged. Much is known about the morphology of the British species and little is to be gained by collecting them. Dead specimens quickly lose their colouration and aesthetic appeal; there can be little justification other than for bona-fide scientific purposes.

Recording dragonfly behaviour and their habitats

It is always worth carrying a still or video camera when watching dragonflies in the field. Their bright colours and array of behaviour lend themselves to photography. Modern photographic equipment, both film and digital, can be used to produce pin sharp portraits of dragonflies with relative ease. Photography also enables one to record details of dragonfly habitats and evaluate changes over time (see section on conservation). Good field notes describing the date, time and direction should accompany each habitat photograph.

Dragonflies are highly mobile insects with good visual acuity and are easily disturbed by a careless approach. They require a fair degree of patience to photograph them successfully. Most species are active during warm, sunny conditions and this can provide a challenge to the best of photographers. Under these conditions a close approach requires stealth and care. In dull, cool conditions they are somewhat easier to approach but do not exhibit the behaviour that makes them such a fascinating group of insects. Dawn can be a good time to photograph dragonflies, when they rest motionless in the vegetation waiting for the warmth of the sun. This is a very atmospheric time of day, enabling use of the superb lighting conditions.

A camera fitted with a short telephoto or zoom lens, in the range of 70-200mm, is good for most species photographs. A macro lens (in the range of 90-200mm) allows pin sharp focussing from infinity to life size, enabling the photographer to fill the frame with a small damselfly. A wide-angle lens in the range of 17-35mm is useful for portraying some species in their surrounding habitat. Setting the focussing ring to the hyperfocal distance on the lens greatly increases the depth of field and enables the insect to be photographed in its habitat. Fixed focal length wide-angle lenses usually outperform the wide-angle zooms in their close focussing ability.

One needs to be ready for action at all times, as opportunities often arise which require rapid reactions, especially when wishing to photograph behaviour.

Approaches to dragonfly photography involve the use of available light or flash. Very rarely if ever can dragonflies be photographed successfully in available light using a hand held camera unless one uses fast shutter speeds or a lens with image stabilisation. A good sturdy tripod and head is essential for available light photography. This enables the creative photographer to utilise the available light conditions to portray the dragonfly as naturally as possible. Active dragonflies under windy conditions make this approach especially frustrating. Flash photography enables the photographer to hand hold the equipment with freedom of movement. Flash photography however can be unpredictable with light from the flash being reflected as highlights from the dragonflies' wings. It can also produce an unnatural black background, as if the subject had been photographed at night. In combination with available light the careful use of 'fill in' flash can be useful to add a touch of sparkle to an otherwise flat subject.

Video cameras, especially the current digital versions, open up new possibilities for recording dragonfly behaviour not possible with still photography. High speed filming followed by slow motion playback reveal many fascinating aspects unseen by the naked eye.

The species photographs in this book were taken with Canon EOS 3 & 5 cameras fitted with EF100mm or EF180mmL macro lenses. An EF20mm wide-angle was used to portray species in their natural habitat and EF24-85mm or EF17-40Lmm zooms were used for general habitat shots. Gitzo 320 and 1228 tripods fitted with a Foba Superball head were used for available light photography to provide steady support. The Gitzo 1228 is constructed from lightweight carbon fibre and provides a welcome saving of weight when walking large distances on foot.

References
[1] See glossary

[2] P. Trodd (pers.com.)

[3] Prince and Clarke (1993)

[4] Palmer (1950b)

[5] Dijkstra et al (2002)

[6] Anderson and Anderson (2002)

[7] Moore (2002)

[8] Cham (1993)

[9] Cham (1991)

[10] Appendix 1

◀ Banded Demoiselle photographed at 5.45 am along the backwater at Kempston Mill, July 1998. This is an atmospheric time of day when dragonflies remain motionless at their roosting sites.

Flight periods of Damselflies (Zygoptera)

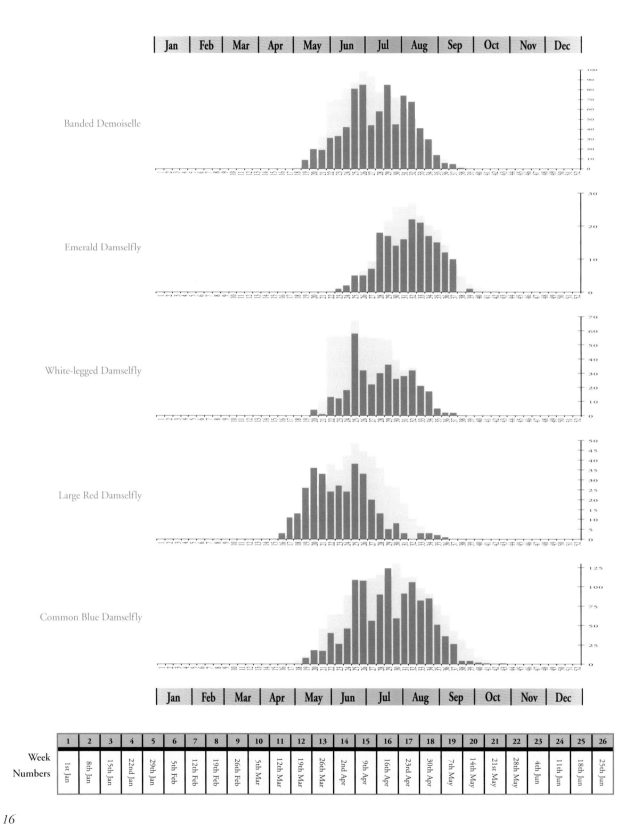

N.B. Each histogram shows the flight period for Bedfordshire in dark green, overlying the national flight period in light green. The number of records on the vertical axis only applies to Bedfordshire records. Week numbers represent the week starting on the day given at the bottom of the page.

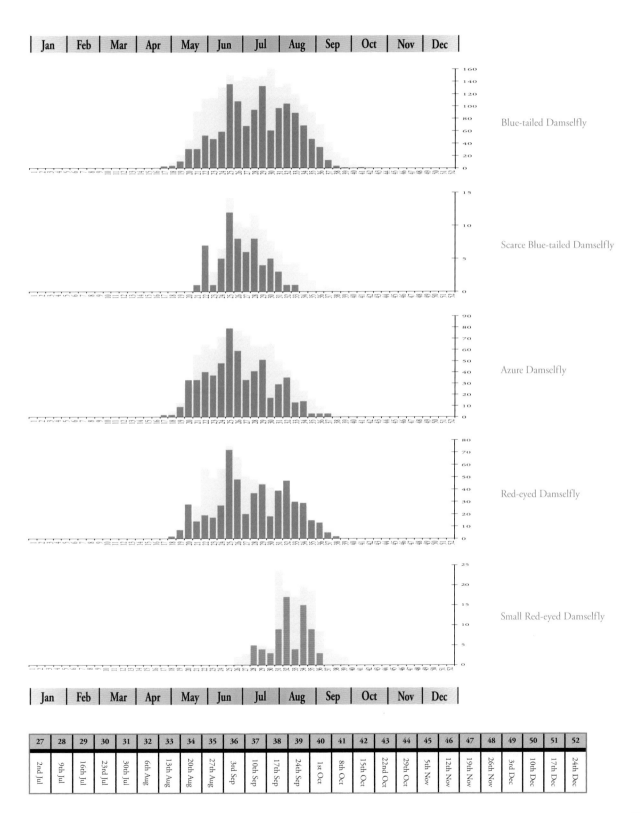

Flight periods of Dragonflies (Anisoptera)

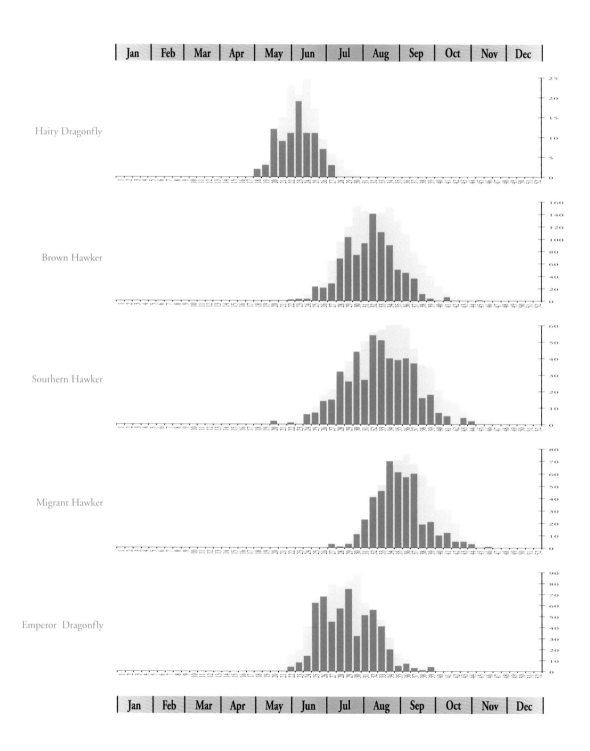

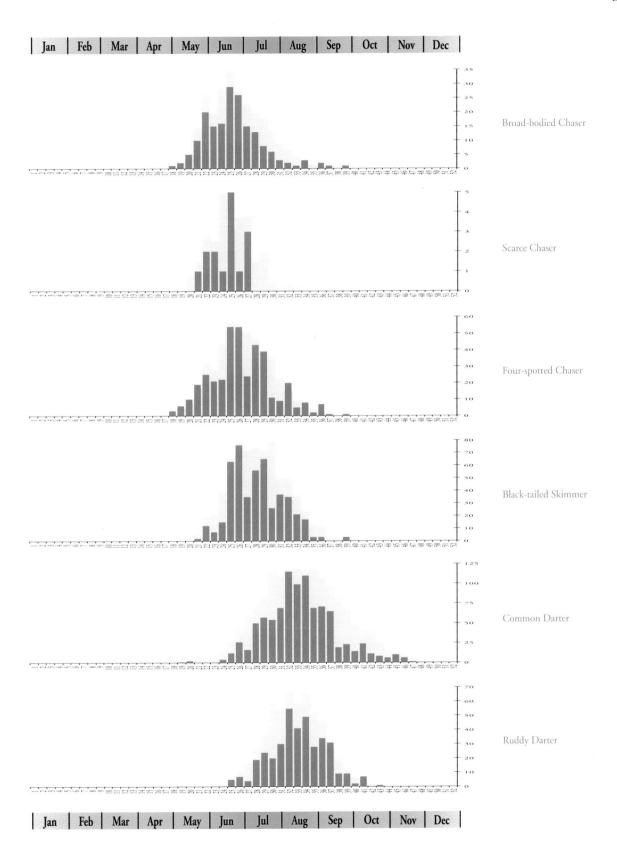

Dragonfly recording in Bedfordshire

Entries in "Lepidoptera Anglica cum Libellulis[1]"

Libellula grandis (=*Aeshna grandis*) "Ford End August 1797. My own garden Aug 23 1798".

Forcipata -(in another hand *Cordulegaster annulata* (=*Cordulegaster boltonii*). "J.C. Dale took one in Clapham Park wood"

Anquis (= *Aeshna cyanea*) "Common Aug 1797".

Area (*puella?* in another hand) (*Agrion puella* =*Platycnemis pennipes*) "Ford End - Common September 1797".

Vulgata ? (added in pencil) Harris. (=*Sympetrum striolatum*) "Common Aug 1797".

Entries from JC Dale's "calendar"

1818 July 1 "♀ *Aeshna viatica* nr. Bedford".

1819 July 13 "Clapham Park Wood" "♂ and ♀ *Agrion corea* in great plenty".

1819 July 14 "on ye River Ouse" [among other insects noted]: *Calopteryx Ladovicea*" (=*C. splendens*), "*Agrion Corea* in plenty".

1819 July 16 "*Agrion Annulare* (=*Coenagrion puella*) between Potton and Gamlingay".

1820 May 31 "*Libellula conspurcata* (=*Libellula fulva*) Newnham Bedford Mr Bucklow brought me".

1820 June 1 "Clapham Park Wood" *Gomphus vulgatissimus* [among other insects noted].

Compared to the Lepidoptera and other insect groups, the dragonflies of Bedfordshire had received little attention from entomologists until relatively recently. This situation is similar to many other counties, including neighbouring Hertfordshire: *"This is an order that has been much neglected by entomologists, compared to the ever popular Lepidoptera and Coleoptera"* (Hine 1934).

The early years

(pre-1940)

The Reverend Charles Abbot (1761-1817) was perhaps the first person to notice dragonflies in Bedfordshire. He had a keen interest in the Lepidoptera and Odonata of the county, which he recorded in his notebook "*Lepidoptera Anglica cum Libellulis*"[1]. This small notebook of about 240 pages is with the Dale papers in the Hope Library, University of Oxford Museum and contains several entries on dragonflies (see side panel). Abbot's contribution to the entomology of Bedfordshire has been reviewed by Charles Baker elsewhere[2]. Mr Bucklow of The Swan Inn, Bedford, bought Abbot's collection of insects, which included a number of dragonflies, for four guineas. Bucklow then sold it in 1817 to J.C.Dale who also acquired "*Lepidoptera Anglica cum Libellulis*". J.C.Dale was a renowned entomologist and passed through Bedfordshire whilst travelling between Dorset, where he lived, and Cambridge where he was at university. He visited several sites in the county, mainly for butterflies, but also noted dragonflies.

The first published record for Bedfordshire, which was of Scarce Chaser *Libellula fulva* from Newnham, Bedford, appeared in the first handbook of British Dragonflies by W.Harcourt Bath[3]. This is most likely the specimen acquired from Mr Bucklow by J.C.

Dale and noted in the calendar. This record is also the only record from Bedfordshire quoted in Lucas' '*British Dragonflies*'[4] which was perhaps the first successful handbook on the subject and stimulated interest in the group. The records in Dale's calendar for Golden-ringed Dragonfly and Club-tailed Dragonfly are puzzling, as these species no longer occur within flying range of Bedfordshire. Were they misidentified or were habitats in the county suitable for them in the early 1800s but deteriorated later? Unfortunately we know few if any details of the habitats or water quality in the streams and rivers at that time.

The Victoria County History (VCH) volumes are often a good source of records for insect groups. Surprisingly there are no records for dragonflies in the VCH for Bedfordshire[5], which further indicates the paucity of effort at the time.

Hertfordshire also seems to have had few naturalists specialising in dragonflies, Stephens in 1836 mentions just four species for the county[6] :

Aeshna mixta (*affinis*)
Aeshna grandis
Anax imperator (*formosa*)
Brachytron pratense (*A.vernalis*)

These records are again repeated in several later publications[7,8,9]. Subsequent papers by Palmer[10,11] list 18 and 25 species respectively for Hertfordshire although Gladwin later disputed some of these records[12]; "*It is now known that the records of some rare species are the subject of error*". The records for Migrant Hawker are particularly interesting. At this time the species was considered to be only a migrant. Some of the unconfirmed records of Common Hawker in atypical habitats in Bedfordshire and Hertfordshire at this time may have been this species as the two are easily confused.

The first Bedfordshire Natural History Society recorders

(1940-1970)

The present Bedfordshire Natural History Society was formed in 1946 and since that date several individuals have acted as county recorders for the Odonata. Ray Palmer, who lived in Flitwick from 1942, became the official recorder for the Bedfordshire Natural History Society between 1946 and 1950. He stimulated interest in dragonflies in the county and communicated and received records from B.B.West and D.W.Snow of Bedford, B.Verdcourt of Luton and D.A.Reid of Leighton Buzzard. Miss Cynthia Longfield provided details of Bedfordshire records obtained whilst preparing the second edition of her book[13] and also helped to confirm identification for some county records[14].

About the same time period, Mrs J.M.Adams[15] was recording in Bedfordshire and listed 14 species. She did not appear to be aware of the activities of other recorders.

In 1951 after Palmer stepped down as recorder, the father and son combination, Kenneth and Bernard West, shared the recording activities in the county over the next decade; K.E.West 1952-3, 1959-63 and B.B.West 1954-8. Both wrote reports in the Journal of the Bedfordshire Natural History Society. The 1959 edition the annual report[16] concluded:

"it would appear that this field of study as far as the county is concerned has been fairly well covered".

Recent recording

(1970- present day)

In Bedfordshire the concept of mapping the distribution of animals and plants on a 2km square (tetrad) grid was first advocated by J.G.Dony and pioneered by him in his plant atlases [17,18,19] for Bedfordshire and Hertfordshire. It was *"possible to express more concisely.... the distribution of a species within a given area"*.

Dr Nancy Dawson became county dragonfly recorder in 1972 and started the process of recording the distribution of dragonflies on a tetrad basis. She reviewed the county's species at the time, comparing them with the earlier records of Palmer[20]. Bedfordshire had seen many changes to its dragonfly habitats since the first reference to the group in the literature more than a century ago. In the absence of field guides during the early 1970s Nancy set about producing an illustrated hand coloured key to stimulate interest amongst the county's naturalists[21]. In the report of the recorder for 1981[22] she discusses the 'best' sites in Bedfordshire. They were all open, shallow and sunny with plenty of vegetation in the water and around the edges. During her fifteen years as recorder she published annual reports in the *Bedfordshire Naturalist*. She was able to report the discovery of the Scarce Blue-tailed Damselfly in her final year as recorder[23].

One of the most significant publications on the county's natural history was '*Bedfordshire Wildlife*'[24], which provided a comprehensive review of the county's natural history. It refers to the White-legged Damselfly, Ruddy Darter and Broad-bodied Chaser as being on the limit of their British range in Bedfordshire and in decline nationally. This however was in error as both the White-legged Damselfly and Ruddy Darter were already undergoing significant recovery and range expansion by 1987 and have continued to do so to the present day.

▼ Publications of the Bedfordshire Natural History Society covering Dragonflies

The author took over as county recorder in 1988. In the same year the Bedfordshire Biological Records Centre was set up as part of a national network of local records centres. This has been run as a joint venture between the Natural History sections of Bedford Museum (North Bedfordshire Borough Council) and Luton Museum (Luton Borough Council). A provisional atlas of the dragonflies of Bedfordshire[25] was published soon after to encourage further submission of records. The tetrad distribution maps at this time reflected more the effort of recorders than the true distribution of the county's dragonflies. The 1990s saw more Bedfordshire Natural History Society members involved in recording dragonflies as more field guides became available.

In recent years more emphasis has been placed on establishing proof of breeding and recording on a site basis rather than tetrads. Proof of breeding is especially important as it confirms that a site is capable of supporting the complete life cycle of a species. When sites are at risk from development, or conservation measures need to be implemented, detailed records maintained in a database can be of great value. With the increased recording effort and the introduction of computerised recording it is appropriate to record at a more detailed level. Modern database and mapping software enables species records to be quickly retrieved and analysed. In addition to distribution maps for each species, it is also possible to use coincidence mapping to show the main 'hotspots'

for assemblages of dragonflies, and thus used to identify important areas of the county (see pages 44-46).

Computerisation of Bedfordshire records

All dragonfly records for Bedfordshire are maintained in a computerised database. A customised version of the BioBase recording software, known as DARTER, has been used to input all records for the county from 1817 to the present day. Records are conveniently entered using an interface that mimics the RA70 recording card. Data can easily be retrieved and analysed, by site or species, using conventional database tools.

All Bedfordshire records are passed on to the Dragonfly Recording Network (DRN) in electronic format. The DRN maintains a national database of records used to assess the status and distribution of dragonflies in Britain. One of the main aims and objectives of the recording scheme is to provide high quality data that will help to conserve British Dragonflies and their habitats. The DRN is run by the British Dragonfly Society in collaboration with the Biological Records Centre at Monks Wood and feeds data into the National Biodiversity Network. Data can be retrieved by conservation agencies and naturalists via the NBN gateway website (Appendix 6). This ensures that data is mobilised quickly and is available when required by conservationists.

References

[1] Abbot, C. (MS)

[2] Arnold *et al* (1997)

[3] Bath (1890)

[4] Lucas (1900)

[5] Doubleday and Page (1904)

[6] Stephens (1836)

[7] Evans (1845)

[8] Bath (1890)

[9] Lucas (1900)

[10] Palmer (1930)

[11] Palmer (1940)

[12] Gladwin (1997)

[13] Longfield (1937)

[14] Palmer (1947)

[15] Adams (1945)

[16] K.E.West (1959)

[17] Dony (1972)

[18] Dony (1967)

[19] Dony (1976)

[20] Dawson (1976)

[21] Dawson (1977)

[22] Dawson (1982)

[23] Dawson (1988)

[24] Nau *et al* (1987)

[25] Cham (1990a)

▶ RA70 recording card and DARTER software have been the standard means of recording dragonflies for a number of years. The card enables six life stages to be recorded with an estimate of the numbers present. Each stage is entered into DARTER directly from the card details.

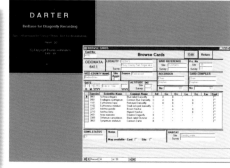

Dragonfly habitats in Bedfordshire

The egg and larval stages of all British dragonflies require clean freshwater habitat for their development. The adult stages require suitable wet areas in which to breed, as well as surrounding areas that provide an adequate supply of insect prey and shelter. This hinterland is an important, yet often overlooked element of a dragonfly's habitat requirements. It can influence the numbers of breeding dragonfly species present however good the aquatic habitat. A landscape, which promotes varied freshwater and terrestrial habitats will attract a greater variety of dragonfly species. The freshwater habitats in Bedfordshire today fall broadly into two main categories; running water and stillwater.

For a small county, the Bedfordshire landscape is particularly varied. The surface relief of the county is dominated by three upland ridges, which cross the county in a south-west to north-east direction. The chalk downs in the south of the county form the highest relief (243 metres near Dunstable Downs) and they dip away to a Gault Clay vale as one moves north, rising again on the central ridge of Lower Greensand. Continuing north the land again drops to Oxford Clay before rising again to the Great Oolite Limestone in the north of the county. The low-lying areas of the Oxford clay form the River Great Ouse valley which, along with its tributaries, drains much of the northern part of the county. A full review of the Bedfordshire Landscape is given in 'Bedfordshire Wildlife'[1].

With the exception of rivers there are no natural areas of open water in the county. All the present stillwater bodies are man-made. The history of the wetlands of Bedfordshire is not well documented, although there is some evidence to suggest that many wetland habitats have been lost. Until the 17th Century the wetlands of the Great Ouse Valley would have provided continuity of marshland habitat between the county and the vast marshland habitat of the Fens [2]. The floras of Abbot[3] and Saunders[4] refer to sites in Bedfordshire, such as Ampthill Bogs and Potton Marsh, that have long since been drained and converted to agriculture. Dony[5] noted that the vast majority of native plants lost in the county during the past two centuries have been from

Habitat surveys

When carrying out site assessment or habitat management for dragonflies, a number of key factors need to be considered:

- **Water depth** - influences the water temperature and penetration of light and thus the development of water plants and invertebrates.
- **Aspect** - determines warmth of a site; south facing sites warm more quickly and are more attractive to dragonflies.
- **Surrounding vegetation** - provides a shelterbelt of trees especially on the north and west sides, which will protect a site from cold winds. It can also have the opposite effect by shading the water surface and reducing temperature.
- **Submerged vegetation** - provides larval microhabitat and oviposition sites and is a general indicator of diversity. The type and structure of submerged plants can be important for some species.
- **Emergent vegetation** - provides perches for territorial males and attracts females to oviposit (e.g. Hairy Dragonfly requires dead floating stems for oviposition). Dense stands of emergent vegetation are important for some species whereas others prefer open conditions.
- **Hinterland** - provides sheltered feeding and maturation areas for dragonflies near to the breeding site.
- **Proximity of other dragonfly sites** - can be a source of potential colonisers.
- **Water quality** - can be affected by nearby source of chemicals/enrichment/pollution.
- **Potential threats** - can come from nearby development/disturbance.
- **Management history** - the success (or lack) of previous site management.

marshes and water meadows. The loss of such habitat would have had significant impact on dragonflies. The large-scale drainage and canalisation of the rivers isolated wetland habitat into smaller fragments until we are left with the situation we see today.

Shallow water generally supports a richer ecosystem than deeper conditions and provides the best dragonfly habitat. Temperature, by controlling metabolism, affects almost every activity of dragonflies[6]. The warmer habitat conditions provided by a south-facing aspect and the penetration of sunlight encourage growth of submerged vegetation and micro-

invertebrates, which in turn determine the 'attractiveness' to dragonflies. Submerged vegetation provides suitable microhabitat conditions in which the larvae can live and is also essential for some adults to oviposit. Emergent and marginal vegetation are also important for females of some species to oviposit. Male dragonflies perch and hold territories in these areas, as they are the areas that are most attractive to females.

Surrounding woodland and trees play an important role for some species by providing feeding or mating areas. Trees are also important in providing shelter, especially from northerly and westerly winds. Trees with a dense leaf canopy can however cause heavy shading of the water surface as well as leading to an accumulation of leaf litter, which can have a negative impact. For some dragonfly species such as the Downy Emerald *Cordulia aenea*, the presence of extensive surrounding woodland appears to be an essential criterion in habitat selection. The lack of such habitat in Bedfordshire may explain the absence of this species.

For most British species relatively little is known about the microhabitat conditions that favour one species over another. There are examples of species occurring in neighbouring counties, but absent in Bedfordshire. The lack of sites for the Variable Damselfly in Bedfordshire is surprising, as significant populations occur at the River Great Ouse valley gravel pits at Huntingdon and St.Ives, some 15km from the county boundary. At these sites the species occurs in very high numbers in early summer, usually outnumbering the closely related and more common and widespread Azure Damselfly. It is not known why this should be so and why similar habitats in Bedfordshire do not support the species.

Finally, it should be remembered that most habitat types go through a succession of changes. This is especially true of stillwater sites. From the moment a pond, lake or quarry site is created, colonisation

▼ Map showing the location of significant rivers, streams and canals in Bedfordshire.

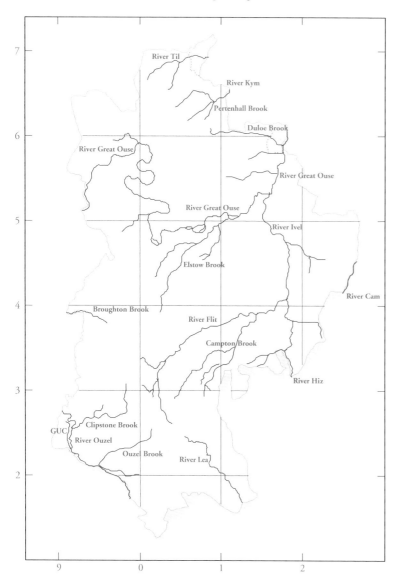

by vegetation commences. Without habitat management the vegetation in general will become more dense and lush. These successional changes also influence the dragonflies present and a change in the mix of species will occur over time. A good example of this is provided by the Common Blue Damselfly, which favours sites with plenty of open water and minimal vegetation. In contrast the Ruddy Darter requires lush stands of emergent vegetation with little open water surface. This is an important point to bear in mind when site management work is carried out and if a site is to support a range of species.

Running water

Bedfordshire rivers and streams are generally of good water quality and support a range of dragonfly species wherever suitable habitat exists. The distributions of species such as Banded Demoiselle and White-legged Damselfly are largely restricted to running water. On a visit to the River Great Ouse on an warm day in June or July one can see high numbers of male Banded Demoiselles holding territory along the banks and out over the water. This species is almost ubiquitous to clean flowing water and its absence under suitable weather conditions for activity is highly suggestive of a problem with water quality. One would also expect the distribution of White-legged Damselfly to be similar, but in fact it shows a much more restricted pattern. This is largely due to differences in the structure or 'architecture' of bankside vegetation. In areas where there has been bankside disturbance or clearance this will be one of the first species to disappear.

All the rivers in Bedfordshire have been modified by human intervention at some time over the last century. This has resulted in the loss of valuable wildlife habitat, with water meadows in particular having disappeared from the river valleys. Bedfordshire rivers

are monitored for water quality by the Environment Agency and water quality data for all Bedfordshire rivers can be found on the Environment Agency's website[7]. In general the number of breeding species increases with increased water quality.

River Great Ouse

The River Great Ouse is without doubt the most significant river corridor in the county. Its existence has influenced the formation and development of many of the county's best dragonfly sites. It rises near Brackley flowing through Buckinghamshire (VC24) to enter Bedfordshire at Turvey in the northwest of the county. It then follows a winding

▲ The River Great Ouse at Turvey as it enters Bedfordshire from Buckinghamshire. A good site for Banded Demoiselle and White-legged Damselflies.

▼ The River Great Ouse upstream from where it leaves the county at Wyboston. Despite the river being navigable to pleasure craft this stretch supports White-legged and Red-eyed Damselflies as well as the county's only known population of Scarce Chaser.

course of some 50 km eastwards towards Bedford and then on to Wyboston where it flows into Huntingdonshire (VC31). The upper reaches, west of Bedford are of a more varied nature and rich in wildlife. Dony[8] regarded the Upper Ouse Valley to be "*scenically and botanically…. one of the more interesting parts of the county*".

Downstream of Bedford the river becomes sluggish and follows an almost straight course as it flows through intensively farmed land and some of the flattest parts of Bedfordshire. This is in sharp contrast to the upper reaches. Many stretches have been straightened and water controlled by weirs to provide easier navigation for pleasure craft. It is now possible to travel by boat from Bedford to the North Sea.

Up to the early 1980s the Anglian Water Authority (AWA) undertook an extensive programme to 'improve' the county's rivers. Along the River Great Ouse east of Bedford there was extensive straightening of the water course, making it uniform depth, often removing islands, making steep sides and reducing marginal vegetation. Such measures had a severe effect on breeding bird populations along the rivers[9] and dragonfly numbers appear to have suffered similarly. Dawson[10] reported that White-legged Damselfly was "*not recorded downstream of Bedford since*

AWA canalised the river". This species is particularly susceptible to disturbance of bankside vegetation. In 1980 the Water Space Amenity Commission published its Conservation and Land Drainage Guidelines showing how improvements could be made without producing such a negative impact on wildlife. AWA adopted these guidelines and the river began to regain its dragonfly interest. The amount of boat traffic on the River Great Ouse has increased considerably in the last few decades since the river was made navigable between Bedford and the Wash. Despite the increased turbidity of the water the impact of boat traffic appears to have had less effect than the riverside bank alterations. Today the White-legged Damselfly occurs in high numbers along the navigable stretches of the river as it flows through Bedfordshire and into Huntingdonshire wherever bankside vegetation is suitable.

Rivers Flit, Hiz and Ivel

In the southeast of the county the Rivers Ivel and Hiz enter the county from Hertfordshire (VC20) joining together near Henlow. The River Flit flows into the River Ivel as the Ivel Navigation at Langford, which then flows northwards to join the River Great Ouse at Tempsford. These three rivers flow through intensively cultivated land, much of which is flat and low lying. Many of the hedges and trees in these valleys have been removed to create larger fields and more productive agriculture. The loss of such habitat has had a negative impact on insect populations, which in turn provide a food resource for dragonflies. In addition, agrochemicals used in the area have inevitably found their way into the rivers. For many years the numbers of dragonflies had not been as high along these rivers compared to the River Great Ouse. It is interesting to note that Dony[11] regarded the River Ivel to be inferior to the River Great Ouse and recorded that the White Water-Lily which was "*common along the Ouse*"

During the 1940s "the Ouse was a very different river with lots of dense aquatic vegetation and very good bank vegetation. During the war and for some years afterwards it was not much interfered with". Similarly the River Ouzel "was a very clean river then."

(B.Verdcourt pers.com.)

▼ River Ivel, Beeston, adjacent to active gravel working. The river banks have experienced disturbance over the years which has resulted in extensive growth of Common Nettles in places. August 2002.

was apparently absent in the Ivel. This is an important plant for some riverine dragonflies and would have had some effect on species such as Red-eyed Damselfly, which favour the floating leaves.

The River Ivel has improved considerably over the last decade with a dramatic increase in the variety of species now present. Notably, White-legged Damselfly has colonised the river from the River Great Ouse during the mid to late 1990s, reaching as far as the River Flit at Chicksands. During the late 1990s the Ivel valley was designated as a linear Water Park and attracted considerable conservation effort. This has benefited some stretches of the river which have been made more attractive to dragonflies. Other parts of the river still demonstrate the effects of past bank clearance. The resulting dense growths of Common Nettles remain virtually devoid of dragonfly interest.

The Elstow Brook

This small stream rises in the heart of brick country in the Marston Vale. It flows north towards Bedford and then east to join the River Great Ouse at Willington. The brook serves as a corridor for riverine species. Banded Demoiselle breeds in most years with adult males dispersing into surrounding areas. Somewhat surprisingly, White-legged Damselfly started to colonise the brook during 1999 being recorded along the stretches with lush marginal vegetation as far as Kempston Hardwick. The Brook flows for most of its length through agricultural land and is visibly of variable quality. It regularly suffers interference in the form of bank clearance and water abstraction and this results in lower water levels and duckweed in the slower reaches, which reduces its potential for dragonflies.

River Kym

Flowing mainly through Huntingdonshire the River Kym has a short stretch in Bedfordshire, which attracts Banded Demoiselle and a few

other species. It is not until it flows east of Hail Weston outside the county that it becomes a suitable river to support breeding populations of dragonflies.

River Ouzel and Ouzel Brook

The River Ouzel rises as the Ouzel Brook near Dunstable sewage treatment works and flows west through arable land towards Leighton Buzzard. The river forms the county boundary with Buckinghamshire for some of its length and then flows parallel with the Grand Union Canal through Leighton Buzzard. The river continues on through Milton Keynes, eventually flowing into the River Great Ouse near Newport Pagnell in Buckinghamshire. During the 1940s White-legged Damselfly was noted as common along the River Ouzel, especially near Rushmere, Heath and Reach. Over the years the river suffered from development and bank clearance and dragonfly numbers crashed during the 1960s as water quality and bank habitat deteriorated. At one time the Otter *Lutra lutra* was also reported to be common in the area which suggests that the water was of good quality. Although current management practices are more sympathetic, some stretches of the river still undergo radical clearance of bankside vegetation.

The section north of Leighton Buzzard is the best for Dragonflies with

▲ The River Ouzel at Grove. The lush bankside vegetation provides ideal habitat for Banded Demoiselle and White-legged Damselflies.

good numbers of Banded Demoiselle in most years. The White-legged Damselfly appears to have recovered but is restricted to the well-vegetated stretches in Bedfordshire. Along the Buckinghamshire stretch high numbers can be seen each year and these provide a source for future recolonisation.

The Broughton Brook is a small stream that flows into the River Ouzel at Milton Keynes. It offers limited attraction to dragonflies, but supports small numbers of Banded Demoiselle along the Bedfordshire stretch. Similarly, the Clipstone Brook flows from Tingrith through Hockliffe, joining the River Ouzel at Leighton Buzzard. The stream flows through agricultural land and has little dragonfly interest mainly due to low water quality.

Grand Union Canal

The Grand Union Canal has a short length in the south-west of the county where it runs near to the River Ouzel. Its waters become turbid due to the amount of boat traffic using the canal and along many stretches the banks are either boarded or concrete. Despite this, marginal vegetation has established a foothold in places and supports a range of species including Banded Demoiselle and White-legged Damselfly. Dragonfly numbers are largely supplemented from the River Ouzel and nearby quarry sites where they breed.

River Cam

The River Cam rises as the River Rhee at Ashwell in Hertfordshire and forms the eastern Bedfordshire county boundary for a short distance south of Wrestlingworth. This stretch is subject to various interference from agriculture, especially bank clearance, and has limited interest. It does however support small numbers of Banded Demoiselle.

River Lea

The River Lea rises at Leagrave Marsh (now Marsh Farm) in Luton, flowing through the town to leave the county at East Hyde. Due to their linear nature, rivers in urban areas are likely to acquire runoff and pollutants from various sources. Much of the river becomes regularly silted and is of low quality. *"It (the River Lea) was once an attractive stream, but has become badly affected by the growth of Luton."* [12] During some years Common Darter and Migrant Hawker have been observed along the river margins but they are wanderers from elsewhere. *"It is a much fouled river which leaves Luton."* [13] As the river leaves Luton it widens to form the lakes at Luton Hoo, which also suffer from the same silting and water quality problems. The River Lea at East Hyde carries a high proportion of road drainage and treated sewage effluent. As a result there is only a very short stretch of the river as it crosses into Hertfordshire that is attractive to dragonflies, mainly small numbers of Banded Demoiselle.

Stillwater sites

Open standing water is an increasingly common and widespread habitat in lowland Britain due to the flooding of former mineral workings and the construction of reservoirs. A habitat survey in 1990 showed that 0.7% of the county's land area was standing water.

Mineral workings that create

▼ Willington Gravel Pits in August 2002 provides a diversity of habitat types for dragonflies, such as the Black-tailed Skimmer and Common Blue Damselfly.

stillwater habitat fall into three main types: Sand/Gravel, Chalk and Clay. Each type has created pools that have their own characteristics and differing attractiveness to wildlife. The most important difference between them is water depth, which can restrict light penetration, and establishment of submerged plants. In most lowland waters there is little plant growth below 2 metres. Emergent plants will colonise shallows down to a depth of 1.5 metres which is especially noticeable in the larger flooded clay pits. Most of these sites are 3 metres or deeper which restricts their potential for plant growth and utilisation by invertebrates. The flooded brick pits around Stewartby, in the Marston Vale are much the deepest.

The range of species that are attracted to mineral extraction sites is influenced by their stage of development. When newly excavated, all mineral workings have large areas of bare earth and limited vegetation. At this stage of succession they support a limited number of species, which typically includes Common Blue Damselfly and Black-tailed Skimmer. As vegetation gains a foothold other species are attracted in. At the other extreme a site may take several decades before it is suitable for the Scarce Chaser to colonise.

Sand and gravel pits

The extraction of sand and gravel for the building industry has been carried out for centuries. The abundance of gravel along the county's river valleys has inevitably led to its exploitation. Valley gravels are present along the Ouse, Ouzel, Flit and Ivel valleys with former workings at Blunham, Cople, Felmersham, Harrold/Odell, Langford, Radwell, Priory, South Mills, Willington and Wyboston. More recently new workings have been developed in the Ivel Valley at Broom and Sandy and the Willington complex has been extended, creating many new pools.

During the Second World War

gravel was extracted at Felmersham to provide material for the runways at Thurleigh and Cranfield airfields. The construction of the M1 motorway and Milton Keynes further increased the demand. Formerly, the extraction of gravel was carried out in narrow bands, which left a ridge and depression pattern. As they became flooded they formed the finger lakes, which are a prominent feature of some of the older gravel pit sites such as Felmersham, Priory and Cople. In the Great Ouse valley the colonisation of flooded gravel pits by vegetation and invertebrates can be relatively rapid due to the proximity of the river. During flood conditions the rivers spill over into the gravel pits carrying viable parts of plants and dragonfly eggs and larvae.

Gravel pits a few years after flooding begin to attract species that favour open water and bare banks. Such pits start to develop submerged patches of aquatic vegetation. Aquatic plants such as Canadian Waterweed are quick to colonise new sites and they can form vast underwater carpets. During 2002 the gravel extractions at Beeston had produced pools with an almost total underwater covering of this plant. These conditions are especially attractive to Common Blue Damselflies, which can be seen hovering in high numbers over apparently open water with the plants below. Bare sunny banks at these 'new'

▲ Priory Country Park Finger Lake in July 2003. This is one of the best dragonfly sites in the county. A colony of Small Red-eyed Damselfly breeds in this lake.

In the report of the Bedfordshire Natural History Society dragonfly recorder[15] K.E.West noted: "*The filling in and levelling of old gravel pits must destroy the breeding grounds of some species, but as they are all established in more permanent quarters we have little to fear.*"

"*An important part of the natural history of the county is so greatly influenced by the county's economy.*"[18]

It was noted by Dony that "*there is more open water in the county now than at any period since natural history observation began.*"[14]

sites attract Black–tailed Skimmers with territorial males 'sunning' at intervals around the margins. This behaviour is characteristic of the species.

The gravel pits found along the river valleys show noticeable differences in their ability to support dragonfly species. The more mature extraction pits tend to support more species. Felmersham NR is one of the oldest and ranks as one of the best dragonfly sites in the county. The lakes are of varying depths with varying degrees of shading[16]. This has a significant influence on the plant communities that develop. The middle lake at Felmersham NR has significantly higher numbers of submerged aquatic plants such as water milfoil species and Rigid Hornwort than the other lakes at the site. This is reflected in the range of dragonflies that breed in each lake.

Sand extraction has occurred across much of the Greensand ridge where it crosses the county. At many of the quarry sites the quick draining nature of the rocks does not allow for the formation of standing water. Open water does however occur in sand workings at Leighton Buzzard, Heath and Reach and Sandy. Two small ponds at the Greensand Project reserve at Sandhouse Lane support good colonies of dragonflies. Mermaid's pond at Aspley Guise was formerly a good dragonfly site but became heavily overgrown as the water table dropped due to nearby quarrying.

The extraction of Fuller's Earth at Clophill during the mid to late 1990s led to the creation of lakes when it was flooded at the turn of the millennium. At the time of writing it is too early to determine how the site will develop for dragonflies. The lakes with their bare margins already attract good numbers of the early colonising species such as Common Blue Damselfly and Black–tailed Skimmer.

Chalk quarries

Chalk formations were laid down in the Cretaceous period and form the major escarpment stretching across the south of the county from Whipsnade to Arlesey. The demand for cement for the construction industry led to the establishment of cement and lime works at various points along the chalk. A few of these were sufficiently deep to expose the water table and create areas of open water. Of particular interest are the quarry sites at Houghton Regis and Sundon where shallow spring-fed seepage pools have formed. This seepage habitat is nationally important for one of the county's rarest species, the Scarce Blue-tailed Damselfly.

Houghton Regis quarry was worked pre-war and extended over an area of 71ha. The site was abandoned in 1971 and the adjacent cement works demolished[17]. At this site the lower chalk is underlayed with chalk marl, highly calcareous clay that extends across the quarry. This impervious deposit has allowed the formation of marl lakes, which form the dominant feature of the quarry floor. A deep marl lake is a permanent feature of the quarry but has little plant growth and less to attract dragonflies. A shallow marl lake experiences dramatic changes to its water level. A series of springs emanating from the base of the chalk cliffs and a small spring-fed stream provide the water supply to most of the pools in the quarry. The water supply from these springs can be highly

▼ Houghton Regis Chalk quarry in former times. The shallow pools and seepages supported a range of species including the Scarce Blue-tailed Damselfly. The lack of water reaching the wet areas has resulted in loss of dragonfly habitat. June 1992.

variable. In dry years the lack of ground water entering the aquifer causes the stream and springs to stop flowing. During the 1990s the spring water started to decrease leading to pools drying out across the site. In extreme years such as during 1996/97 the shallow marl lake became totally dry. The aquatic microhabitats vary across the site and attract a range of species if they remain wet. During the summer of 2003 the water levels were again critically low, resulting in the loss of key dragonfly habitat.

Sundon quarry is a larger complex of chalk workings of some 125ha and was also worked pre-war. Working ceased in 1976. In the southern half of the quarry, spring lines emanate from the base of chalk cliffs and feed a series of pools and shallow seepage areas. These vary in their flow and unless the volume is sufficient the pools tend to dry out in some years. The spring lines create flushes immediately below the chalk cliffs, which have provided ideal conditions for the Scarce Blue-tailed Damselfly. In the middle of the quarry a lake complex is the main water feature comprising a series of pools that were formed into one. An adjacent smaller pool has some dragonfly interest including a small breeding colony of Small Red-eyed Damselfly. The northern part of the site is dry and has considerable botanical and lepidoptera interest. It also provides a good feeding area for maturing dragonflies.

The Blue and Green Lagoons at Arlesey comprise smaller chalk quarry sites than Sundon and Houghton Regis. They both have deep pools that limit the range of submerged plants and both have less dragonfly interest.

Clay pits

The Marston Vale, comprising drift deposits overlying Oxford Clay, spans an area between Bedford and the M1 motorway. In past times it had a natural wetland system. The extraction of clay for the brick making industry has dominated this area; centred on

Stewartby it has created a number of significant areas of open water in the county.

In contrast to other workings the clay pits tend to form very deep water. The lakes at Stewartby, Brogborough and Kempston Hardwick are the last to freeze over in cold winters. Vegetation and invertebrates are slow to colonise these sites[19]. The larger expanses of open water create wind-generated waves of sufficient size that inhibit plant growth at the margins. They also create turbidity, damage vegetation and erode the banks. Shallow water is a relatively scarce habitat in the Marston Vale and mainly in the form of small pools, drainage ditches and flooded disused railway lines. These sites are more

▲ Sundon Chalk Quarry, June 2002, showing the shallow water filled wheel ruts that are the breeding habitat of Scarce Blue-tailed Damselfly.

▼ Coronation Clay Pit, with Stewartby brickworks in the background. The site comprises a diversity of different size pools with varying water depths that attract a range of species. May 2002.

▲ Broadwater, Wrest Park, Silsoe 2002. The various lakes form one of the best dragonfly sites in Bedfordshire and support a range of species, including one of the largest populations of Red-eyed Damselfly.

attractive to dragonflies than the bigger lakes.

At Stewartby Country Park the south-east corner of the main lake has been set aside as a protected wildlife area. Here the lake forms a small inlet surrounded with emergent vegetation. A few small pools have also been left between extractions, which are attractive to dragonflies. Habitat creation in the Marston Vale has produced a range of wetland habitat such as pools, scrapes, ponds and ditches. The Marston Vale Millennium Country Park is the most adventurous of these with a visitor centre as the focal point for walks amongst various wetland habitats. At one of the new pools reed beds have been created to attract marshland birds and should also be attractive to dragonflies.

When the clay extraction was in full production small railways were used to move materials between sites. With their demise the tracks were ripped up leaving linear depressions that filled with water. The disused railway line south of Marston Moretaine has created several short wet areas where pools have formed that attract a range of species. The densely vegetated areas support colonies of Emerald Damselfly and Ruddy Darter.

One of the best sites in the Marston Vale is at the north end of Coronation Clay Pit. The site comprises a large deep lake with limited dragonfly interest as well as numerous small pools between the ridges left by the extraction process. This area has become overgrown with scrub which provides ideal conditions for feeding and shelter. The largest population of Large Red Damselfly in the county is found at these pools. Each year in early summer thousands of emerging adults can be seen. The pools also support large numbers of Azure Damselfly as well as Four-spotted Chaser.

Lakes

There are no natural lakes in the county. Artificial lakes have been made on the large country estates, often by damming the flow of streams. The main artificial lakes are in parkland at Southill, Woburn, Battlesden, Old Warden, Wrest Park and Tingrith Manor. During the 1950s Southill lake was "*the largest stretch of still water in the county*"[20]. The lakes at Wrest Park, Silsoe support some of the highest numbers of Azure and Red-eyed Damselfly in the county. Despite a large head of carp in the lakes there are significant areas of submerged and emergent plants that attract dragonflies.

The lakes at Luton Hoo, Melchbourne and Stockgrove are of low quality largely due to the activities of waterfowl. Other lakes of medium size occur at Rushmere, Colworth, Toddington and Flitwick Manor.

On a smaller scale some landowners have created lakes and ponds for fishing that also attract some dragonfly interest. Examples of these can be found at Water End, Maulden and Tingrith.

Road development can sometimes have beneficial spin-offs for pond and lake creation as they make attractive 'fill ins'. Good examples of these can be seen along the southern Bedford bypass where a series of pools and lakes have been created along its length. The industrial distribution centre at Marsh Leys, Kempston has created an ornamental lake as a key feature in front of the buildings and this already has several species breeding.

The difference between lakes and ponds is their relative size. For the purposes of distinction a pond can be roughly defined as an area of water one can throw a stone over.

Ponds/Moats/Ditches

Ponds are important habitats for dragonflies. Recent research has shown that they have a higher total species richness than most other freshwater habitats[21].

Three main factors influence the quality of a pond and its 'attractiveness' to wildlife (including dragonflies):

- Water quality
- Shape and design
- Proximity to other wetlands

Ponds in Bedfordshire can be classified into three broad groupings:

Temporary/seasonal ponds - that dry out for part of the summer. They support specialised plants and animals including some rare British wetland species. Such sites have few species of dragonfly.

Semi-permanent ponds - that dry occasionally. These support species that can develop rapidly such as Emerald Damselfly and Ruddy Darter.

Permanent ponds - that always contain water but levels may fall significantly during the summer.

Water levels in most ponds naturally rise in winter and fall in summer. This creates a drawdown zone which is important for some species. In semi-permanent or seasonal ponds the water dries to damp mud in the summer and becomes colonised with emergent vegetation such as Soft-rush and Common Spike-rush that cover the complete area. A good example of this in the county is a series of ponds that run along the southern wall of Woburn Park. During the summer these ponds have lush vegetation with damp mud and at first appear unsuitable for dragonflies. They do however support healthy colonies of Ruddy Darter and Emerald Damselfly. The female Ruddy Darter oviposits by throwing its eggs into the wet mud and surrounding vegetation whereas the Emerald Damselfly inserts its eggs into plant stems. In both cases the eggs overwinter, awaiting the rise in water levels during the winter period. The hatching of the eggs takes place in early spring with a rapid larval development that enables the adults to emerge in the summer. This rapid development and one year life cycle enables these species to survive the dry period and colonise these seemingly unsuitable sites.

Permanent ponds are also relatively short-lived in historical terms. If left unmanaged plant material and sediments accumulate and rise until the pond becomes a marsh with no open water. Flitwick Moor provides a good example of this where large pools were present and have been lost to vegetational succession.

In former times field ponds were an essential part of livestock farming, until the advent of piped water supplies. There are numerous examples in Bedfordshire where field ponds are now no more than damp hollows. Where they do still exist moderate trampling and grazing by livestock can create a complex of tiny pools providing suitable habitats for a range of invertebrates.

▼ Semi-permanent pond at Milton Bryan on the southern edge of Woburn Park, during late August 2002. Muntjac deer tracks can be seen across the wet mud. Both Emerald Damselfly and Ruddy Darter were ovipositing here on the day this photograph was taken.

▲ Colmworth Golf Course lakes in 2003. The bare margins attract Black-tailed Skimmers while the large expanses of Broad-leaved Pondweed provide ideal habitat for Emperor, Red-eyed and Azure Damselfly.

Village ponds historically, were a source of water for villagers and livestock. They are a feature of a number of Bedfordshire villages. However, they are prone to enrichment from road run-off and the activities of waterfowl and humans. They are also prone to blooms of duckweed and Water Fern. Some village ponds are heavily stocked with fish resulting in turbid water and algal blooms. They have little if any dragonfly interest. Milton Bryan village pond is an example where overstocking of fish, run-off and enrichment from wildfowl has significantly reduced its attractiveness to dragonflies.

Tilsworth pond was created in 1973 and was well studied over several years by Bryan Inns. A range of species was recorded but following construction of the Leighton Buzzard by-pass and improved drainage of the surrounding area, the water table dropped leading to the pond becoming permanently dry.

Golf courses are another provider of pond habitat for dragonflies. With the increased popularity of the sport there can be few courses that do not have some form of water feature as an obstacle on the fairway. Some of these ponds are artificially lined to retain water; others occur in natural hollows. The ponds usually benefit from being in the open and in full sun and the less manicured ones can be attractive to dragonflies. Good examples can be

found at Millbrook and Colmworth Golf Courses.

Trees beside water can have both a positive and negative influence on dragonflies. Where roots and branches enter the edge of ponds they can provide good oviposition sites for some species such as Brown and Southern Hawker. Root growth can also have a negative impact by speeding up the drying out process by drawing up water through transpiration. Ponds in woodland are often shaded and accumulate leaf litter that significantly reduces their attractiveness to dragonflies.

Dony[22] stated "*There are now very few ponds*". However, as more and more landowners develop an interest in the natural world, ponds with wildlife interest are being created. Furthermore, garden ponds are becoming an increasingly important habitat for some species. There can be few ponds that have not at some stage had a visiting Southern Hawker. In the absence of fish and newts, garden ponds can support high numbers of breeding dragonflies. Careful consideration for the needs of dragonflies during the planning stage of pond creation can result in a range of species using it[23].

Where they occur ditches are of some importance as stillwater habitats for dragonflies. The drainage ditch at Marston Thrift has some dragonfly interest. In former years it had significant stretches of open water and supported 11 species. Recently it has become increasingly overgrown and much of it now has little to attract open water species. It does however still support Emerald Damselfly and Ruddy Darter. At Biggleswade Common some of the ditches support good colonies of Azure Damselfly and Blue-tailed Damselfly, but are prone to duckweed blooms covering the water's surface.

Sewage treatment works and farm irrigation lagoons

Sewage treatment works would have formed good habitat for dragonflies before modern methods were incorporated. Bedford sewage treatment works was a well-visited site for its birds before it was modernised and the open lagoons destroyed. At Dunstable sewage treatment works on the other hand, a series of open lagoons have been created which attract dragonflies. Members of the Bedfordshire Natural History Society have been instrumental in habitat creation at the site, which has greatly benefited in its attractiveness to wildlife.

Farm irrigation lagoons and reservoirs are an increasingly important habitat for dragonflies. They are often out in open farmland where very little water is present. They lack marginal vegetation and water levels are prone to considerable fluctuation. They do however support a range of species, especially Common Blue Damselfly and Black-tailed Skimmer, which are quick to colonise this type of habitat. With sympathetic management they can develop increased wildlife interest. There are a number of good examples on the flat agricultural land of the Ivel valley and in the north of the county.

Bogs and fens

Bogs have been features in the Bedfordshire landscape of the past. During the 19th Century an extensive bog system extending from Cambridgeshire into Bedfordshire was known to support colonies of rare species such as Scarce Blue-tailed Damselfly and Small Red Damselfly *Ceriagrion tenellum*, as well as a breeding colony of Natterjack Toads *Bufo calamita*. Each of these species favours shallow water conditions, a habitat type that no longer exists in this area. Small Red Damselfly occurred at Gamlingay bog[24], but became extinct in the latter part of the 19th century. Henslow and Jenyns[25] found the Natterjack in considerable abundance on Gamlingay Heath in 1824. J.Steele-Elliot[26] also noted "*Natterjacks fairly abundant in some water holes of a sand pit in the parish of Sandy*". Palmer[27] also

notes their presence in this area. The RSPB has reintroduced Natterjacks in recent years to shallow scrapes at their reserve at The Lodge, Sandy. It is unlikely however that the bog habitat will be recreated to enable these damselfly species to re-colonise.

At present, bogs are to be found at only two sites in Bedfordshire. At Wavendon Heath a series of three ponds was formed in 1914, by damming a stream and springs as a catchment for water on the rapidly draining Greensand. The acid conditions facilitated bog formation with the colonisation of *Sphagnum* mosses, which formed floating rafts. This site supported a small colony of Black Darter in the 1950s but sadly natural

▲ Farm irrigation reservoir, Bolnhurst in 2003. Although water is abstracted through the pipes in the foreground this site supports a range of species.

▼ Flitwick Moor pools in 2002 shortly after management work to clear encroaching vegetation.

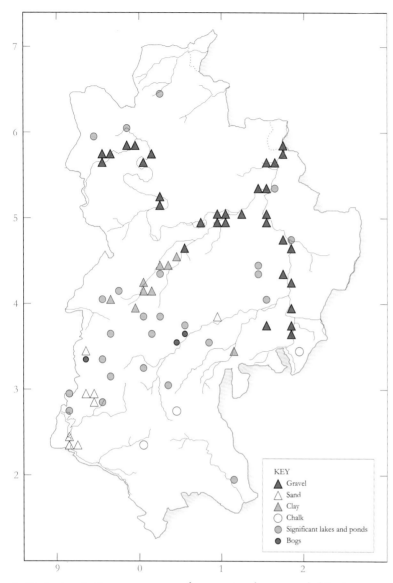

▲ Distribution of stillwater habitats in Bedfordshire.

KEY
▲ Gravel
△ Sand
▲ Clay
○ Chalk
● Significant lakes and ponds
● Bogs

See Appendix 3 for Dragonfly sites with fifteeen or more breeding species.

extraction for local farmland has lowered the water table. By the late 1960s the site was becoming overshaded and water quality was changing; "*Less natural aquatics and semi-aquatics were present*"[29]. Conservation work during the 1990s opened up some of the site and has created small pools. As yet the attractiveness to dragonflies does not match former times. Flitwick Moor provides a good example where pools have been lost when natural succession is allowed to take its course. Even over the last two decades some of the pools have dried out as plant material and sediments have accumulated resulting in a marsh with no open water.

A few kilometres further along the valley is a smaller site on the peat at Flitton Moor. As a nature reserve run by the County Council several ponds and ditches have been created which support a number of species.

References
[1] Nau *et al* (1987)
[2] Nau *et al* (1987)
[3] Abbot (1798)
[4] Saunders (1911)
[5] Dony (1976),
[6] Corbet (1999)
[7] Environment Agency website (see appendix 6)
[8] Dony (1953)
[9] Trodd & Kramer (1991)
[10] Dawson (1980)
[11] Dony (1953),
[12] Dony (1976)
[13] Dony (1953)
[14] Dony (1976)
[15] West (1953)
[16] Cham (2002b)
[17] Bedfordshire County Council report (1978)
[18] Trodd and Kramer (1991)
[19] Dony (1976)
[20] Dony (1953)
[21] Williams *et al* (1997)
[22] Dony (1976)
[23] Moore (2002)
[24] Merritt *et al* (1996)
[25] Palmer (1949)
[26] J.Steele-Elliot (1905)
[27] Palmer (1949)
[28] See plate 14 in Dony (1953)
[29] B.B.West (pers.com.)

seral succession has caused this site to gradually dry out and become shaded by surrounding trees. Some attempts at conservation work have failed to have any significant impact. The site still dries out in most years and the dragonfly interest has been lost.

At Flitwick Moor the excavation of peat between 1718 and 1967 allowed the cuttings to become flooded with acidic spring water, which encouraged the colonisation by bog vegetation. During the late 1940s the 'Moor' had numerous bog pools, which provided ideal breeding habitat for dragonflies[28]. The site has been progressively drying out over the last few decades as water

Conservation

Despite a much greater public awareness of wildlife conservation British Dragonflies still face a number of threats to their habitats. Of the forty or more species that originally bred in the British Isles three have become extinct since 1952. Whilst some of the best dragonfly sites in Bedfordshire are protected or managed as nature reserves others are under threat.

The best protected sites in Bedfordshire include Felmersham Gravel Pits which are managed by the Wildlife Trust, Wrest Park by English Heritage, Harrold-Odell and Priory are managed as country parks. In contrast some important SSSIs (Sites of Special Scientific Interest) at the mineral extraction sites at Sundon and Houghton Regis are under the threat of development and neglect.

If one is to protect key dragonfly habitat in Bedfordshire access to good quality site data is essential. The study of dragonflies can generate many useful records. The many notes and records that are acquired by naturalists should be submitted to a recording scheme where they can be put to good use. If insufficient attention is given to the conservation of freshwater habitats our natural history will be poorer as a consequence. One of the main aims of any recording scheme therefore, should be to provide quality data that can contribute to the management and ultimate protection of dragonflies and their habitats.

Threats to dragonfly habitat

Threats to Dragonfly habitats in Bedfordshire can be roughly attributed to either natural or semi-natural threats and those influenced by humans.

Natural succession
Almost all stillwater habitats in

Bedfordshire have at some time been either created by or managed by human intervention. If these sites are neglected or lack any form of management they will undergo changes resulting from natural plant succession. If allowed to continue they may even be lost altogether. Aggressive colonisers such as Bulrush quickly colonise the shallower margins of pools. As they grow they trap silt between the roots leading to a reduction in open water surface and further plant growth.

Tree growth further speeds up the transition to dry land by drawing up water through transpiration. The increased shading from trees also makes sites less attractive to dragonflies. This is especially a problem when trees block

▼ Flitwick Moor showing the loss of large areas of open water through natural succession. The site was photographed from the same viewpoint in 1986 (bottom) and 2002.

◀ Mermaids Pond, Aspley Guise photographed in 1985 and July 2003 from the same viewpoint. The loss of this site as a good dragonfly site is due to heavy shading of the pond by the growth of surrounding trees. The problem is made worse by the increased uptake and transpiration of water by the trees.

a southerly aspect. One of the major contributing factors to the demise of Wavendon Heath ponds was the virulent growth of Rhododendrons and Birch in the immediate proximity of the ponds.

Water chemistry

Good quality water with low levels of phosphates and nitrates enables the development of a wide range of aquatic plants and associated invertebrates. Water enrichment on the other hand has been responsible for the loss or reduction of aquatic life at a number of sites in Bedfordshire. In some cases the effects have not been significant enough to have an impact on dragonfly numbers.

Pollution is regarded as an imbalance between the input and outflow of substances that is large enough to cause biological impact[1]. Pollution incidents inevitably have an effect on some form of wildlife. Chemical run-off from agricultural land is an ever-present threat. Drainage ditches flowing into streams and rivers from intensive arable land carry high levels of nutrients, which lead to extensive algal blooms, and rafts of duckweed. At some sites the introduced Water Fern can have a similar effect. The River Ivel valley contains some of the best farmland in the county; much of it classed as Grade 1 by DEFRA. Intensification of farming in these high-grade areas has resulted in loss of hedgerows, abstraction of water from the river, run-off and aerial drift of agrochemicals. Drainage from intensive arable land often contains high levels of nutrients that cause algal blooms.

Water quality is an important influence especially on the wildlife of shallow lakes. Where nutrient levels are high there is a risk of algal blooms that reduce light penetration and restrict plant growth to all but the shallowest areas.

Urban development leads to habitat destruction, further compounded by industrial effluents and road construction. Run-off from roads is a major cause of silting and chemical enrichment. The liberal use of salt during icy periods finds its way into the watercourses. The River Lea with its source at Marsh Farm in Luton becomes heavily silted and polluted from run-off. It is devoid of dragonflies for almost its entire length in Bedfordshire.

During the early part of March 2003 local newspapers carried a story of the potential threat posed by landfill sites. Heavy rainfall over the winter period caused water levels in the brick pits at Elstow to rise to the point of

◀◀ Houghton Regis Chalk Quarry SSSI photographed looking north in July 1990 (top) and July 2003. The loss of most of the shallow pools has had a significant impact on the dragonfly populations. The disappearance of the Scarce Blue-tailed Damselfly is directly attributable to this. The arrows indicate the shallow pools and seepages where it once bred.

▼ Milton Bryan village pond in 2003, suffers enrichment from waterfowl and road run-off. A road drainage pipe can be seen in the foreground. The result is a widespread algal bloom that excludes all other aquatic plants.

▲ Harlington Village pond completely dry during summer 1990.

overflowing into a pool containing toxic waste leachate. This raised concerns about it getting into the lakes and affecting wildlife.

Drought/water abstraction

Lack of water through natural drought is a cyclical phenomenon and affects a number of sites in the county. During 1976 the Wavendon Heath ponds and some of the ponds at Cople Pits dried out completely during the dry summer. Water levels also fell significantly during the 1990s. A period of drought between July and September 1990 saw a number of ponds drying out. Most notable was Harlington village pond and Wavendon Heath ponds again. In the same year, ponds in the Haynes area dried out

▶ Elstow Brook, Cardington, August 2000. Water abstraction for agriculture leads to reduced water flow, lowering of water levels, increased emergent plant growth, duckweed and algal 'blooms'.

completely for only the second time in living memory[2]. During 1997 a number of sites were again without water. The main lake at Houghton Regis was completely dry during the latter part of 1996 and all through 1997. The lake at Cityfield Pit near Henlow which was a good site for dragonflies dried out completely during 1991 and has never recovered its former dragonfly interest. Some small streams also dried out during this time. The summer of 2003 was again very dry with record temperatures for Britain. Many shallow ponds in the county were dry during August and September. The shallow lake in Houghton Regis quarry was dry resulting from a lack of water coming from the springs.

The replenishment of water is an important factor in the permanence of both standing and running water. The lowering of the water table can turn permanent water bodies into temporary ones. Under such conditions dragonfly species with a long development cannot survive. Even running water habitat can be affected if water levels drop too low. Water abstraction reduces water levels and velocity, particularly where rivers and streams flow through areas of intensive agriculture. The Elstow Brook regularly suffers from low water levels creating conditions that encourage algal and duckweed blooms. Marginal vegetation then grows more rapidly resulting in the need for clearance operations and further bank disturbance. Such operations particularly affect the White-legged Damselfly, which has been attempting to colonise the Elstow Brook and is restricted to the lengths with lush bank vegetation.

Alien plant introductions

The introduction of exotic plant species can have a big impact on the ecology of a habitat. One significant threat to ponds across Bedfordshire is the rapid colonisation by the New Zealand Pigmyweed. This small aquatic plant, which has been introduced from garden centres, can quickly dominate to the point at which it excludes other plants more beneficial to dragonflies. Maulden Church Meadow Pond has been described as one of the finest examples of a field pond in the county[3]. The discovery of New Zealand Pigmyweed was made in the mid-1990s and by 2002 was already dominating a major part of the pond. At Poppy Hill the lake margins have dense growth in places. Ponds in other counties are known to have lost their dragonfly interest after this plant has taken over the water's surface[4].

The misguided introduction of Water Soldier into stillwater sites in the county has caused problems when it has become too invasive. These non-native populations reproduce vegetatively and can quickly dominate an area of water. At Harrold-Odell Country Park the wildlife pond was completely covered during the summer of 2002. This was formerly a very open pond with a good range of dragonfly species but had gradually become taken over by Water Soldier and Common Reed to the point at which the dragonfly interest has diminished. It is also present at the Finger Lakes at Priory Park, but has not caused a major problem. This may be due to parts of the site being shaded and regular removal of plants. At the time of writing the lakes at Felmersham Gravel Pits have increasingly large patches. There have been attempts to remove the Water Soldier from some of the lakes by hauling plants out onto the bank to rot. Whilst this can become an onerous and ongoing task, the rotting piles do create good habitat for Grass Snakes (*Natrix natrix*).

The main conservation lesson for site managers is to remove alien plant species at an early stage and not to allow them to gain a foothold.

Drainage/neglect

There have been many examples of the loss of habitat through deliberate destruction or neglect. In Bedfordshire most of the former

▲ Harrold-Odell Country Park wildlife pond in 2002. This area of water's surface is completely covered with Water Soldier.

bogs have been drained and water meadows prevented from flooding in winter. The latter resulted from the programme of canalisation of rivers for flood management, which particularly affected the River Great Ouse. Many field and farm ponds have been lost due to neglect following the switch from pastoral and mixed farms to tillage. Sites become overgrown and shaded if trees and bushes are allowed to grow naturally without management.

Landfill

Much of the Marston Vale between Bedford and the M1 motorway has been associated with the brick industry for many years. As working clay pits it is inevitable that brick pit sites will change in time. At a number of these sites water has been pumped out in preparation for landfill, with the loss of dragonfly habitat. In 1989 landfill operations started draining the pools at Brogborough No2 pit. By the following year the habitat for dragonflies had been lost. In former years shallow pools with emergent vegetation provided ideal conditions for dragonflies. These areas held some of the highest numbers of Emerald Damselfly and Ruddy Darter ever recorded in the county. During 1999 the southern part of Rookery pit was reworked and drained with the loss of many small pools and ditches that were good for dragonflies.

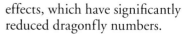

▲ Brogborough landfill has resulted in the loss of dragonfly habitat. Some pools survive on the fringes.

References

[1] Corbet (1999)
[2] D.Parsons (pers. com.)
[3] Revels (2000)
[4] Author's observations
[5] Driver (1997)

▼ Conservation work to remove shading trees and bushes from the gravel 'fingers' at Felmersham Nature Reserve, during the winter 2002/3 .

Recreational use

The increased interest in fishing as a major recreation has led to the creation of new lakes and ponds in the countryside. Although such wetland creation may seem to be beneficial to dragonflies it can also have a negative side. High densities of fish adversely affect dragonfly numbers by direct predation on larvae as well as creating turbidity and enrichment that prevents plant growth. Extensive 'weed' clearance to create free fishing swims reduces aquatic vegetation. This is often self defeating as it destroys the food chain on which both larval dragonfly and fish development are dependent. The use of aquatic weed killers at some sites in the county has been responsible for chemical imbalance and pollution

effects, which have significantly reduced dragonfly numbers.

Recreation activities such as water skiing and power boat racing not only lead to the risk of diesel and oil spillage but the waves generated by the boats leads to erosion of banks and water turbidity. These activities are restricted to the larger lakes in the county such as Stewartby and Wyboston, which are less attractive to wildlife as a result.

Habitat creation and management

Landowners can contribute to the conservation of dragonflies by either managing existing aquatic habitats or creating new ones. Whilst dragonflies benefit from most conservation activities aimed at aquatic habitats they have received special attention in some areas. In Britain there are two dragonfly sanctuaries specifically for the conservation of British species: one at Ashton Water, Northamptonshire and the other at Waltham Abbey, Essex. In comparison, Japan has at least 24 such reserves dedicated to dragonflies.

Conservation work parties can make significant improvements to aquatic habitat especially by removing shading trees, encroaching Bulrush and other invasive species. At Felmersham Nature Reserve the Wildlife Trust has directed workparties at removing encroaching trees on some of the small islands that form the fingers across the lakes. This has opened up more light into important areas for dragonflies. Similar tree clearance and removal of encroaching Bulrush at Duck End Nature Reserve, Maulden has significantly improved its attractiveness to dragonflies.

The Marston Vale Millennium Country Park at Marston Moretaine has created a number of water features including ponds, lakes and ditches.

Heritage Lottery Funding for the Millennium village pond at Eversholt is a good example of how habitat can

be created. Opened in June 2002 this village pond was already supporting a range of breeding species.

Balancing ponds have been created in some urban areas to assist with land drainage. Examples of such ponds can be found at Cut-throat Meadow, Ampthill and Saxon Pond, Biggleswade. Such ponds can be attractive to dragonflies where the water quality has not suffered from enrichment. Where water quality is poor a reed bed may provide some uptake of nutrients before water enters a pool[5]. At the Interchange Retail Park near Bedford the retention of a pond to aid drainage has attracted a range of species including the Small Red-eyed Damselfly. This pond has dense aquatic plant growth, including Rigid Hornwort which this species favours.

Flooding from rivers can have various effects. It can lead to the dispersal of dragonfly larvae as well as topping up nearby lakes and ponds. During April 1998 and January 2003 extensive flooding occurred along the River Great Ouse. This replenished water in many dried out ponds and ditches. At Felmersham the water levels following the flooding were at their highest in the lakes for many years. This created some new potential breeding areas for dragonflies.

Where cattle have access for drinking the new growth of many plants is highly palatable and eaten. Trampling also helps to keep emergent plants in check otherwise periodic management is essential to maintain open water. At Sundon Chalk Quarry unofficial access by four-wheel drive vehicles and motorbikes is a mixed blessing. On one hand it is regarded as undesirable and can lead to habitat destruction, whereas on the other it is effective in maintaining an open habitat by reducing plant colonisation. The wheel tracks created at Sundon Chalk Quarry have led to water-filled ruts that have been colonised by Scarce Blue-tailed Damselfly.

As habitats are created a wide range

of submerged and emergent plants will colonise naturally. To increase the diversity and the range of habitats for dragonflies it may sometimes be desirable to give nature a helping hand by planting additional species. This needs to be done with great care to ensure that aggressive alien species are not imported by mistake. Some commercial outlets of aquatic plants still give poor quality advice on plants, especially for garden ponds. The hinterland around freshwater habitat needs to be considered in site management plans. Even the best aquatic habitats are less attractive to dragonflies if there is a lack of suitable feeding areas and shelter nearby.

▲ The Interchange Retail Park, Bedford, August 2003. The retention of this pond as part of the land drainage scheme has benefited wildlife. The expanses of Rigid Hornwort at this site have attracted the Small Red-eyed Damselfly to breed.

▼ Eversholt village 'millennium' pond 2003 is a good example of pond creation through local initiatives.

Species Distribution Mapping

The publication of the national *Atlas of the Dragonflies of Britain and Ireland*[1] provided a 'snapshot' of the then current understanding of the distribution of dragonflies. The distribution data for each species is presented in the atlas as dot maps plotted on a 10 km grid. This provides the reader with a visual impression of their spatial distribution.

Simple distribution mapping of species is usually displayed at three resolutions, depending on the geographical area covered. These are typically 10 km, 2 km (tetrad) or 1 km (monad). Species mapping for most plant and animal groups in Bedfordshire has previously been carried out on a tetrad (2 km) basis. This provides a higher resolution map than the 10 km map with more detail for the geographical area of a county. John Dony was the first to pioneer the use of tetrads in Bedfordshire for the recording of plants[2]. There are 249 whole tetrads

covering the county with a further 132 with part of their area in the county. The tetrad map offers a compromise in what it displays. For dragonflies a tetrad map will usually portray a species as visually more abundant than it really is. Therefore, the use of 1 km mapping is to be preferred for county mapping. However, more accurate mapping requires sufficient recording coverage if the map is to show a fair representation of a species distribution. With insufficient recording a map would merely show the distribution of recorders and give the impression of under-abundance. This becomes more evident at higher resolutions. For smaller counties such as Bedfordshire, recording coverage can be achieved over a relatively shorter period of time in comparison with larger counties.

A useful enhancement of the 1km resolution map is to centre the dot over the actual locality where the record was made rather than on a grid. This forms the basis of displaying site related data and is far better at showing associations between a species and its preferred habitat. The comparisons of distribution maps for Banded Demoiselle (see opposite) illustrate the differences of mapping resolution and the effect they have on ones perception of abundance.

Distribution maps - Some words of caution!

A certain degree of caution needs to be exercised when interpreting distribution maps. There are limitations in what the maps show, resulting from the way in which the records were collected. County recording schemes usually and quite understandably collect records in an 'ad hoc' fashion and on a 'what can be got basis'[3]. Records are typically collected during casual walks in the countryside or as a result of concerted effort to record a site in detail. These methods inevitably lead

▼ National coincidence map for all British Dragonfly species. As one progresses northwards from the south coast so the number of species decreases. The arrow points to the centre of Bedfordshire.

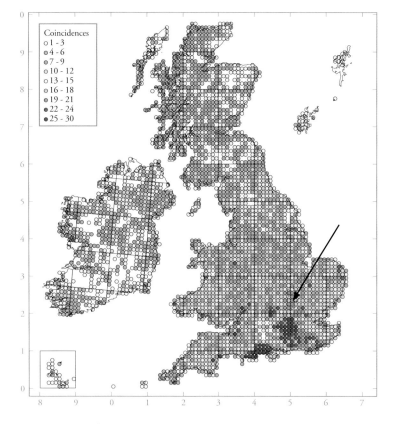

Coincidences
- 1 - 3
- 4 - 6
- 7 - 9
- 10 - 12
- 13 - 15
- 16 - 18
- 19 - 21
- 22 - 24
- 25 - 30

Mapping the distribution of Banded Demoiselle:

The Banded Demoiselle breeds in running water habitat such as rivers, streams and canals. Therefore, a species distribution map should reflect an association with these linear habitats. The maps above show the effect of using different resolutions on the visual perception of abundance.

The 10 km distribution map masks the underlying pattern and is clearly not suitable for showing anything other than presence at a county level. The 2 km (tetrad) map shows a vague pattern developing, but it is still too coarse to show any strong association with the rivers. Whilst being a popular resolution for county mapping the tetrad map can be very misleading. The 1 km map based on a monad grid shows a distribution pattern associated with the rivers. Finally when the dots are centred over the actual location a strong association with the rivers is evident. This type of map can become confusing particularly when dot density is high. It is best used to show simple distribution. For clarity purposes the 1 km map based on the grid provides the best compromise for county dragonfly recording.

Coincidences
○ 1 - 2 (139)
○ 3 - 4 (82)
○ 5 - 6 (77)
○ 7 - 8 (60)
○ 9 - 10 (53)
○ 11 - 12 (48)
● 13 - 14 (23)
● 15 - 16 (26)
● 17 - 20 (13)

▲ Species distribution maps can be combined to show the coincidence of one or more species and thus the 'hotspots' in the county. (The numbers in brackets are the total number of 1km squares where the coincidence range occurs).

References

[1] Merritt et al (1996)

[2] Dony (1976)

[3] Rich (1998)

also influence the number of records for species that fly at the start or end of the adult flight season. Casual observations tend to under record the early appearance of Large Red Damselfly in April. Early records tend to be from those recorders who have deliberately been out to search for them.

The experience of the recorder will also introduce bias in recording. For some species it is necessary to know their jizz and in what type of habitat to look for them. Lack of familiarity with habitat requirements can sometimes result in some species being overlooked. For example, visitors to Sundon Quarry looking for the Scarce Blue-tailed Damselfly often overlook the seepage areas where it occurs and concentrate their searching in the lake area, to no avail.

Accessibility of sites is another factor introducing bias in recording effort. Private sites with restricted access are usually under-recorded compared to public sites. Similarly, remote field ponds are visited less often than sites close to roads and footpaths. Country Parks that offer a 'good day out' offer good accessibility and are often popular amongst recorders.

Finally, distribution maps tend to hide short-term change. The cumulative collection of records will tend to show a species increasing its distribution, even though it may be declining locally. Maps record presence and not absence of a species. The latter can be especially difficult to determine as it will depend on optimal weather conditions during a site visit for some species to be active. A given species may not be recorded on the day due to poor weather even though it is present.

Bedfordshire is a well recorded county and the maps, shown under the species accounts that follow, are a fair reflection of the distribution of the county's dragonflies.

See Appendix 3 for table of Dragonfly sites in Bedfordshire with more than fifteen species.

to bias and uneven recording coverage and may result in a map showing the distribution of active recorders more than the dragonflies.

The amount of time and effort spent recording at a site varies enormously, and again can influence the appearance of a distribution map. Naturalists in general tend to visit 'hot spots' unless specifically requested to visit less popular sites. Some tend to record only on their local patch. These factors will bias the number and type of species recorded. For example, short visits miss some of the larger species such as Broad-bodied Chaser, which tend to 'wander' once they disperse away from their breeding sites. Time of year will

Species Accounts

For the species accounts that follow, information is provided under the following headings:

Distinctive features

Highlights the main identification features along with possible confusion with other species. This is not intended to be a definitive list and is no substitute for a good field guide.

Favoured habitat

An overview of the main habitats where the species is likely to be found, both in Bedfordshire and further afield. Extra detail is given for key species.

Bedfordshire: past and present

Reviews the distribution of the species in the county along with historical records. Where relevant, reference is made to surrounding counties to put the Bedfordshire records into context.

Conservation status

This short section highlights any special conservation measures that may be required to ensure the survival of this species. For rare species that occur in the county additional information is given.

Field notes

Describes interesting aspects of behaviour that often go unnoticed by the casual observer. Wherever possible these are backed up with notes from Bedfordshire observations.

Flight period

Briefly gives the flight period along with first and last dates. This information should be used in conjunction with the flight period histograms in an earlier section (p16-19). NB. Extreme dates may fall outside the normal range.

Bedfordshire distribution map

For each species a 1 km distribution map is used to show the highest estimate of numbers recorded from a locality or site in Bedfordshire during a site visit. The estimates of numbers are based on the ranges used on the RA70 recording card (see p11). This provides a much better visual impression of where the strong colonies for a species are located. (See earlier section on 'Mapping the distribution of Banded Demoiselle at different resolutions').

The key to each Bedfordshire distribution map varies according to the species. This reflects the differences in the numbers one would reasonably expect to find during a site visit. For example, the maximum count of Common Blue Damselfly at a site may number thousands, whereas a Southern Hawker may only ever be seen in ones or twos.

National distribution map

To put Bedfordshire in a wider context a 10 km map is also included to show the species' national distribution. The information used for this map is based on data in the Dragonfly Recording Network's national database. The maps are based on those in the 'Atlas of the Dragonflies of Britain and Ireland'[1] supplemented with more recent records. The dark dots represent records from 1975 to the present day. The lighter dots are for earlier records where a species has been lost from that location.

Looking to the future

Distribution dot maps represent a snapshot in time. Dragonfly surveys should ideally be repeated every 10-15 years to determine changes in distribution. Hopefully, the information and maps in this book will provide any future scheme with just such a snapshot.

Adult abundance on the distribution maps:

The species distribution maps display the highest estimate of numbers made at a locality, on a single site visit, during the recording period (1988-2003). The largest dots show where the strongest populations are to be found.

For some records the number of adults present was not recorded and these have been mapped as unknown.

Mapping breeding status on distribution maps:

Whilst it would be desirable to plot maps showing the breeding status of the county's Dragonflies, the low number of records, providing proof of breeding, would result in a misleading picture. Breeding maps for four common species in appendix 5 are shown to illustrate this point and can be compared with those in the species accounts.

Reference
[1] Merritt et al (1996)

Check List of British Species

Order ODONATA

Sub order ZYGOPTERA (Damselflies)

Family Calopterygidae

Beautiful Demoiselle	*Calopteryx virgo*	N
Banded Demoiselle	***Calopteryx splendens***	**B**

Family Lestidae

Emerald Damselfly	***Lestes sponsa***	**B**
Scarce Emerald Damselfly	*Lestes dryas*	H
Southern Emerald Damselfly	*Lestes barbarus*	N (M)
Willow Emerald Damselfly	*Chalcolestes viridis*	N (M)

Family Platycnemididae

White-legged Damselfly	***Platycnemis pennipes***	**B**

Family Coenagrionidae

Large Red Damselfly	***Pyrrhosoma nymphula***	**B**
Norfolk Damselfly	*Coenagrion armatum*	E
Northern Damselfly	*Coenagrion hastulatum*	N
Irish Damselfly	*Coenagrion lunulatum*	N
Southern Damselfly	*Coenagrion mercuriale*	N
Azure Damselfly	***Coenagrion puella***	**B**
Variable Damselfly	*Coenagrion pulchellum*	H
Dainty Damselfly	*Coenagrion scitulum*	E
Common Blue Damselfly	***Enallagma cyathigerum***	**B**
Red-eyed Damselfly	***Erythromma najas***	**B**
Small Red-eyed Damselfly	***Erythromma viridulum***	**B**
Blue-tailed Damselfly	***Ischnura elegans***	**B**
Scarce Blue-tailed Damselfly	***Ischnura pumilio***	**B**
Small Red Damselfly	*Ceriagrion tenellum*	N

B	**Confirmed as currently breeding in Bedfordshire**
H	Historical record
M	Migrant
N	Never recorded in the county
E	Extinct in UK

Note: Please refer to the contents (pages *III & IV*) for the order of species under the species accounts.

Sub order ANISOPTERA (True Dragonflies)

Family Gomphidae

Club-tailed Dragonfly	*Gomphus vulgatissimus*	H

Family Aeshnidae

Azure Hawker	*Aeshna caerulea*	N
Southern Hawker	***Aeshna cyanea***	**B**
Common Hawker	*Aeshna juncea*	H
Migrant Hawker	***Aeshna mixta***	**B**
Brown Hawker	***Aeshna grandis***	**B**
Norfolk Hawker	*Aeshna isosceles*	N
Green Darner	*Anax junius*	N (M)
Emperor Dragonfly	***Anax imperator***	**B**
Lesser Emperor Dragonfly	*Anax parthenope*	N (M)
Vagrant Emperor	*Hemianax ephippiger*	M
Hairy Dragonfly	***Brachytron pratense***	**B**

Family Cordulegastridae

Golden-ringed Dragonfly	*Cordulegaster boltonii*	H

Family Corduliidae

Downy Emerald	*Cordulia aenea*	H
Northern Emerald	*Somatochlora arctica*	N
Brilliant Emerald	*Somatochlora metallica*	N
Orange-spotted Emerald	*Oxygastra curtisii*	E

Family Libellulidae

Broad-bodied Chaser	***Libellula depressa***	**B**
Scarce Chaser	***Libellula fulva***	**B**
Four-spotted Chaser	***Libellula quadrimaculata***	**B**
Black-tailed Skimmer	***Orthetrum cancellatum***	**B**
Keeled Skimmer	*Orthetrum coerulescens*	N
Black Darter	*Sympetrum danae*	H
Yellow-winged Darter	*Sympetrum flaveolum*	M
Red-veined Darter	*Sympetrum fonscolombei*	M
Highland Darter	*Sympetrum nigrescens*	N
Ruddy Darter	***Sympetrum sanguineum***	**B**
Common Darter	***Sympetrum striolatum***	**B**
Vagrant Darter	*Sympetrum vulgatum*	N (M)
Banded Darter	*Sympetrum pedemontanum*	N (M)
Scarlet Darter	*Crocothemis erythraea*	N (M)
White-faced Darter	*Leucorrhinia dubia*	N

Banded Demoiselle

(Harris 1782)

Calopteryx splendens

Family: *Calopterygidae*

Distinctive features

The Banded Demoiselle is one of Britain's largest damselflies. The blue-black 'band' on the wings and metallic deep blue body of the males makes it a distinctive and easily recognised damselfly. The flight is often described as butterfly-like and gives the species a characteristic jizz.

The females have metallic emerald bodies and greenish wings with a distinctive white pseudo-pterostigma.

Both the adults and larvae of this species can be confused with the closely related Beautiful Demoiselle.

▲ Female Banded Demoiselle 'sunning' itself. This individual clearly shows the white pseudo-pterostigma on the wings. River Great Ouse, Oakley, June 2003.

Favoured habitat

The Banded Demoiselle occurs widely throughout Bedfordshire and is found along all of the main rivers and streams, as well as the Grand Union Canal. It favours slow flowing rivers and streams with muddy bottoms, especially with open banks and adjoining meadows. In years when population densities are high, males will disperse along small streams and ditches and if water levels are sufficient it will attempt to breed. It has been recorded at some stillwater sites in the county, although breeding at such sites has never been proven and is unlikely. Wandering males are occasionally encountered in woodland well away from water, either during the maturation period or as they disperse in search of new sites.

Bedfordshire: past and present

It is widely distributed throughout southern England, East Anglia and the Midlands. Records indicate that it has always been a common damselfly in Bedfordshire. Hine[1] recorded it as fairly numerous along the rivers in

Hertfordshire and also notes that it was numerous along the old canal (Ivel Navigation) at Shefford, Bedfordshire. Palmer[2] stated that it was common along rivers and their main tributaries throughout the county.

▶ Male Banded Demoiselle orienting its body to absorb maximum warmth from the low early morning sun. River Great Ouse, 7.00am, June 1997.

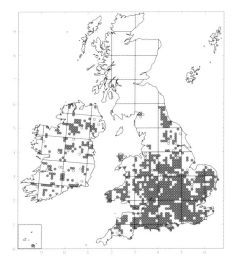

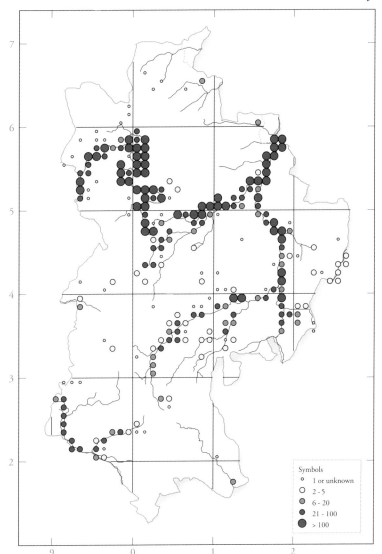

Along the River Ouse at Olney on the Buckinghamshire/Bedfordshire border numbers were regarded as so high during some years in the 1940s and 50s that the species was referred to as the 'blue mist' by the late Gordon Osborne[3]. He remembered blue clouds over the River Great Ouse at Olney during his childhood years. In the 1950s it was "*Common throughout the Ouse valley, less so in the Ivel*"[4].

The distribution map clearly shows the association with the main rivers and streams. The highest population densities occur along the River Great Ouse where it has always been an abundant species. Records away from running water usually indicate wandering individuals.

Conservation status

A proven breeding species in the county. The cleanliness of rivers, streams and canals is of importance to this species. The species' continued absence from a river where the habitat looks favourable is usually an indication of poor water quality.

Field notes

Banded Demoiselles have a characteristic butterfly-like flight resulting from the dark wing banding. They are often seen 'flittering' over water and bankside vegetation. The males are territorial and can occur at very high population densities,

especially along the River Great Ouse. The males often settle on floating vegetation such as Water-crowfoot where females are most likely to

Symbols
- ○ 1 or unknown
- ○ 2 - 5
- ◉ 6 - 20
- ● 21 - 100
- ● > 100

◀ Male Banded Demoiselle displaying to the female whilst in tandem. The vibrating of wings is a precursor to mating. This form of courtship is thought to make the female more receptive to the male's attempts to copulate. Kempston Mill Backwater, June 1996.

they either pick off vegetation or catch in flight. They will perch to consume their prey.

The larvae are relatively easy to find amongst submerged roots and vegetation along the river banks. Larvae are most active at night. Development usually takes two years. Emergence takes place on upright vegetation close to the water's edge. Both larvae and exuviae are very distinctive. The first segments of the antennae are long, sticking out from the head and giving them a horn like appearance.

The closely related Beautiful Demoiselle has never been recorded in Bedfordshire but occurs at various sites in Buckinghamshire and Northamptonshire, including the upper reaches of the River Great Ouse.

Flight period

In Bedfordshire it typically has a flight period from mid May to mid September with some outside this range in exceptional years.

First date   3rd May
Last date   17th October

▲ Male Banded Demoiselle feeding on a Mayfly that it has just caught flying over the river at Oakley, May 2003.

▶ Male Banded Demoiselle holding a favoured vantage point on the backwater at Kempston Mill, July 2000.

oviposit. They attempt to defend a patch of vegetation in prime areas and will actively pursue the females as they fly through their riverside territories. The 'chase' is a memorable sight and demonstrates the intense competition that exists amongst males. There is a form of pseudo-courtship in this species whereby the male displays to the female. During tandem formation and copulation the male vibrates its wings in order to make the female receptive to his attempts to mate.

Copulation lasts between 60-90 seconds during which sperm removal and transfer takes place[5]. Females oviposit in a variety of submerged plants such as the leaves of Water-crowfoot and floating leaves of other plants. Females frequently submerge completely to lay their eggs, which take approximately 14 days to develop and hatch.

Banded Demoiselles can be found roosting overnight in large numbers in bankside vegetation. During periods of bad weather they will often select Common Nettle beds in which to rest. Both sexes have been observed feeding on Alder Flies *Sialis lutaria* and Mayflies *Ephemera danica* which

References

[1] Hine (1934)

[2] Palmer (1947)

[3] G.Osborne (pers.com.)

[4] K.E.West (1958)

[5] See glossary

Beautiful Demoiselle

(Linnaeus 1758)

Calopteryx virgo

Family: *Calopterygidae*

Distinctive features

The Beautiful Demoiselle can be confused with the closely related Banded Demoiselle. The blue metallic colouration on the thorax and abdomens of males is very similar. The wings are distinctive and have a much greater expanse of blue colouration.

The female is metallic green with the wings suffused with a coppery-brown colour.

Any sighting in Bedfordshire should be carefully documented and ideally, backed up with a good quality photograph.

▲ Male Beautiful Demoiselle photographed in the New Forest, Hampshire, May 1998. The wings are completely blue-black and lack the banded appearance of the previous species.

Favoured habitat

The Beautiful Demoiselle favours fast flowing streams with clean stony or sandy beds. It tends to be present along stretches where there are overhanging trees and appears to be more shade tolerant than its close relative. Females are attracted to oviposit where beds of submerged plants, such as Water-crowfoot, grow.

The favoured habitats of the two species are distinctive and only along short stretches of rivers and streams do the two coincide. A visual assessment of the habitat should give the observer some idea which species to expect.

Bedfordshire: past and present

The Beautiful Demoiselle has never been recorded in Bedfordshire. It is included here because of its continued presence along the headwaters of the River Great Ouse, near Brackley where it forms the county boundary between Buckinghamshire, Northamptonshire and Oxfordshire. In this area the species is reported to be on the increase. Records from other counties indicate that it is expanding its range in areas of the east Midlands.

There are some short stretches of streams in the county where the habitat looks favourable and it could turn up should its range continue to extend further.

Field notes

Under bright lighting conditions the wings of male Banded Demoiselles can appear completely blue and this can lead to misidentification. Whenever it has been reported, follow up visits have failed to find the species in the county.

Flight period

The flight period in Britain is usually from the middle of May and lasts until September.

Emerald Damselfly

(Hansemann 1823)

Lestes sponsa

Family: *Lestidae*

Distinctive features

As the name suggests, Emerald Damselflies have a metallic emerald green body. The males have bright blue eyes and develop blue pruinescence on the first and last two segments of the abdomen. At rest adults characteristically perch with their wings held partially open at 45° to their body.

This species can be confused with the Scarce Emerald Damselfly, which has been recorded in Bedfordshire in the past. The latter is a more robust damselfly and must be carefully examined with reference to a field guide.

▲ Male Emerald Damselfly showing the wings characteristically held at 45° to the body. Coronation Pit, July 2000.

Favoured habitat

Emerald Damselflies favour shallow water sites with dense stands of emergent vegetation, especially Rushes and Common Club-rush. Semi-permanent ponds and ditches that often dry out during the summer are favoured sites where it is often found in association with Ruddy Darter. Such conditions are thought to enable larvae to avoid predation by fish. The egg stage overwinters in diapause[1], which enables the species to survive at these temporary waters.

Bedfordshire: past and present

A widely distributed species throughout the British Isles. The scattered distribution across Bedfordshire tends to reflect the specific habitat conditions it favours. The shallow pools that form in mineral extraction sites are where the highest numbers are to be found in the county. At Coronation Pit well vegetated pools have formed between the ridges, created during clay extraction, and these provide ideal conditions. In recent years high numbers have been recorded at

this site from June onwards. During 1988 hundreds were recorded at shallow pools at Brogborough No.2 clay pit, the highest ever recorded for the county. At this time the adjacent Marston Thrift ditch supported equally high numbers. Unfortunately as landfill commenced these pools and ditches were destroyed.

Sandhouse Quarry near Heath and

▶ Pair of Emerald Damselflies in tandem. This male is transferring sperm to his secondary genitalia prior to copulation. Milton Bryan, July 2003.

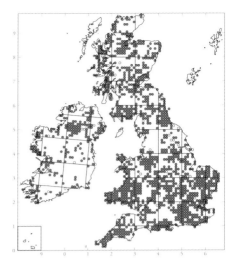

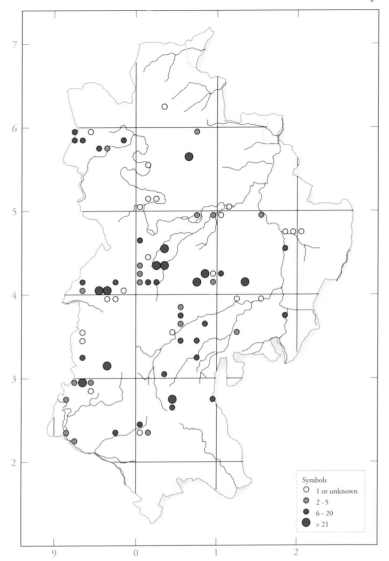

Reach supports a healthy breeding population despite its small size. The ability to survive at sites that dry out during the summer enables it to colonise the shallow pools along the southern edge of Woburn Park near Milton Bryan. Here the ponds are no more than damp mud from July onwards and the damselflies can be seen flying in the dense clumps of Soft-rush along with Ruddy Darters.

In the past it has been less common. Palmer[2] regarded it as "*Apparently rare, I have not taken it in the county and Miss Longfield[3] does not mention it*". It was recorded at Oakley and Great Barford in 1942 by D.W.Snow[4]. It was reported as abundant at Cople Pits 3rd July 1948 and at Wavendon Heath 20th August 1948[5] and frequent at Rushmere Pond, Heath and Reach, Grovebury Pit, Cople and Wavendon Heath[6]. A roadside pond at Milton Ernest was a new locality[7]. Nau[8] recalls it at Green End and Maulden Church Meadow pond in 1987 where they were not present during intense survey work in the mid 1970s.

Conservation status

A proven breeding species in the county. Over zealous removal of dense emergent vegetation during site management can easily destroy the favoured habitat. Accelerated growth of emergent vegetation, especially when water levels are low, favours this species often to the exclusion of others. Habitat management needs to consider the provision of a mosaic of habitat types if this species is to co-exist with other species requiring more open water habitat.

Field notes

Males are territorial but rarely fly over open water. Adults will roost close to water, unlike other damselflies. Mating pairs can sometimes remain in tandem overnight. Early morning visits to suitable sites will reveal many adults perching in vegetation.

Copulation is long, usually taking 30-60 minutes. This can occur in several shorter bouts whilst they

▶ A pair of Emerald Damselflies
'in-cop'. Note how the relative
position of the abdomens change.
During these actions sperm from
a previous mating is removed
from the female, before the male
transfers sperm from his secondary
genitalia[9]. Milton Bryan August
2003.
Note the presence of an egg on the
hind leg of the male, possibly laid
by a parasitic fly.

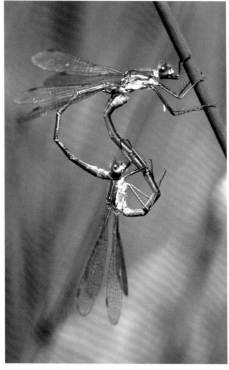

References

[1] See glossary

[2] Palmer (1947)

[3] Longfield (1937)

[4] Palmer (1947)

[5] B.Verdcourt (pers.com.)

[6] Palmer (1950a)

[7] K.E.West (1952)

[8] Nau (1988)

[9] See glossary

remain in tandem. Females oviposit
into emergent stems, often still in
tandem, starting above water level and
then working their way down until
submerged. At semi-permanent ponds
tandem pairs will oviposit low down
in large clumps of Soft-rush. This is in
anticipation of rising water levels during
the winter period. Males fly amongst
these clumps in search of females.

Eggs overwinter in an obligate
diapause. This results in a synchronised
hatching around the onset of spring
followed by rapid larval development,
which can take as little as two months.
The larvae will exhibit active hunting
behaviour as they need to feed rapidly
to complete this development. The
larvae are quite distinctive with

characteristic banded oar-like caudal
lamellae, which they use to swim
vigorously when disturbed.

The closely related Scarce Emerald
may be overlooked due to its similarity
in looks and behaviour. The two
species where they occur together share
similar habitat requirements. It is
worth checking all colonies to confirm
identification.

Flight period
In Bedfordshire it can usually be
seen from early June through to early
September.

First date   31st May
Last date   11th September

Scarce Emerald Damselfly

(Kirby 1890)

Lestes dryas

Family: *Lestidae*

Distinctive features

This species is very similar to the Emerald Damselfly, characteristically perching with wings held open at 45° to the body. It is slightly larger and has a more robust appearance. Identification requires detailed examination of anal appendages and markings of males. In females the vulvar scale of the ovipositor projects beyond the tip of the abdomen. It could possibly be overlooked in Bedfordshire. Suspected sightings should be carefully checked with reference to a field guide.

Favoured habitat

Scarce Emerald Damselfly often occurs at the same sites as Emerald Damselfly and Ruddy Darter, where it favours shallow water sites with dense stands of marginal and emergent vegetation. It breeds in shallow temporary pools, ponds and ditches that regularly dry out in summer. Eggs overwinter in diapause giving it the ability to survive at temporary waters

Bedfordshire: past and present

Nationally rare, recorded on the Kent and Essex coastal marshes and Breckland Pingo ponds. It has always been very local in England and was lost from many sites during the 1950s and 1960s. There were no records at all for the 1970s until it was rediscovered in Essex in 1983.

There has only been one record from Bedfordshire when Drs D.A. Reid and J. Dempster took a single female in July 1950 from a pond at Heath and Reach. This specimen was checked by Cynthia Longfield[1] and notes included in papers in the Longfield/Roberts collection in the Royal Irish Academy, Dublin[2]. Dawson[3] makes mention to Wavendon Heath ponds for this record, but this

was in error. Interestingly, Dr Dempster and Mr M.W. Service recorded a single female on 25th August 1971 at another pond nearby at Rushmere. This initiated further correspondence with Cynthia Longfield, which referred to the earlier record (see side panel). The later Buckinghamshire record was determined by Dr N.W.Moore. The pond referred to in the correspondence lacks these features today. The third pond in the letter is the main lake in Stockgrove Park, which continues to have very little dragonfly interest due to the activities of wildfowl and fish. Derek Reid[4] recalls the pond at Rushmere, where he found his specimen, was very shallow at the time. Such conditions would have been more favourable for emergent vegetation than exist today. These early records are somewhat surprising in that no males were recorded and only single females present.

Conservation status

Whilst not currently recorded in Bedfordshire it could appear in the future if the right habitat conditions prevail. It is on the wing from the end of June through August.

▲ Female Scarce Emerald Damselfly photographed in Essex, July 1981. Note the robust appearance of the abdomen and the large ovipositor.

"Dempster and Reid caught their specimen from the lower of the three ponds within this estate, which was in Bedford. We caught the present female in the middle pond, which is in Bucks. The third pond is most unattractive."

The correspondence went on to describe the site as *"one of the nicest ponds I have seen in years, full of Elodea, Water-lilies, with Typha, Irises around the edges, full of aquatic life."*
(M.W.Service 26.8.1971)

Reference

[1] Palmer (1950a)

[2] R.Merritt (pers. com.)

[3] Dawson (1975)

[4] Derek Reid (pers. com.)

White-legged Damselfly *Platycnemis pennipes*

(Pallas 1771)   Family: *Platycnemididae*

▲ Pair of White-legged Damselflies photographed 'in-cop' at Sundon Chalk Quarry SSSI, July 2003. They have successfully bred at this stillwater habitat in recent years.

Distinctive features

The White-legged Damselfly appears lighter in colour and slightly larger than other blue damselflies. The white laterally flattened feather-like legs, with a black stripe down the middle, are a distinctive feature of this species. The males fly with a bouncy, jerking flight and conspicuously dangling legs, especially in the presence of females.

Both sexes go through age related colour changes where the black markings on the abdomen become increasingly more prominent.

Favoured habitat

The White-legged Damselfly favours unshaded sections of streams, rivers and canals with moderate to slow flow. Areas of lush bankside vegetation with thick herbage are important and this is where the highest numbers are to be found. Tall grasses in nearby meadows are favoured feeding areas. Floating leaves and plant stems and flowers are favoured oviposition sites. In recent years it has been confirmed as breeding at stillwater sites in the county

Bedfordshire: past and present

Nationally its distribution is south of a line from the Wash. In Bedfordshire it is common along the River Great Ouse and in some years it can be the most abundant species present. It also occurs along the River Ouzel and has recently (1990s) started to colonise stretches of the Rivers Ivel, Flit and Campton Brook. It has also been recorded from the Grand Union Canal where it runs close to the River Ouzel. It is very abundant on the River Ouzel outside the county, where it runs through Milton Keynes. This links the Ouzel population in Bedfordshire with that of the River Great Ouse.

Records indicate that this species has undergone major population fluctuations in the past, which appear to be due to major clearance and disturbance of the county's rivers. During the 1940s Palmer reported it to be a common damselfly.

"*Common along the Ouse; often the commonest damselfly; common on River Ouzel near Leighton Buzzard.*"[1] It was "*certainly common along the River Ouzel at Linslade during the 1940s.*"[2]

D.W.Snow who sent records to Palmer reported that "*All along the Ouse where I have looked, from Turvey to Goldington; often the commonest damselfly.*" The records of Palmer from Rushmere Lake, Heath and Reach on 8th June 1950 were most likely

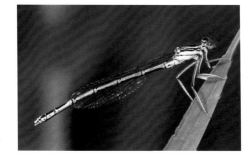

▶ Male White-legged Damselfly clearly showing the laterally flattened legs. Cardington July1998.

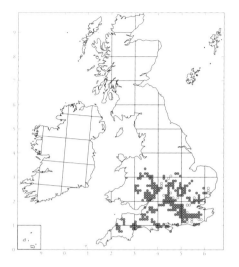

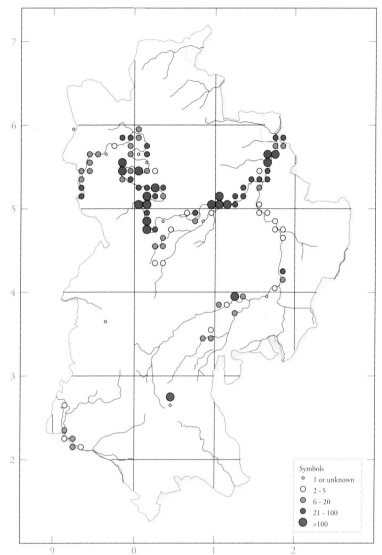

Symbols
- ○ 1 or unknown
- ○ 2 - 5
- ◔ 6 - 20
- ◕ 21 - 100
- ● >100

wandering individuals from the nearby River Ouzel. D. Ashwell reported it as "*common on River Ouzel near Leighton Buzzard, on the Ouse at Bedford.*" "*One sees it in swarms where it occurs, but it cannot be called generally common.*"[3]

Observations recorded in Palmer's notes indicate that sites were visited at slightly different times of the year. He was not aware of the age related colour changes of the species, as he mistakenly regarded the species to have two female forms.

"*On the Ouzel the type and form* lactea *occur in about equal numbers, but* lactea *predominates at Goldington.*"[4]

There were records from the Grand Union Canal, Tring, Hertfordshire in the early 1940s[5] that were most likely an extension of the River Ouzel population. The fate of this colony seems to follow similar observations in Bedfordshire. By 1950 there was a hint that all was not well with the colony at Tring, with only a few seen, "*until recently there was a considerable colony.*"[6]

It was further reported that "*the small colony on the Aylesbury canal near Marsworth found by Bertram Lloyd has apparently not been observed since 1952.*"[7]. This remained the case until it was rediscovered near Tring in 2001, during survey work for the Hertfordshire atlas project[8].

The extensive operations by the Water Authorities along the River Great Ouse during the 1960s and 70s appear to have had a major impact on the species. Along the river its numbers crashed to the point where it was difficult to find. Dawson[9] reported that it had not been recorded downstream of Bedford since Anglian Water Authority canalised the river. During an RSPB

◀ Immature female White-legged Damselfly in the *lactea* phase. Wyboston, July 1998.

▲ Group oviposition on the backwater at Kempston Mill. Along a short stretch of this small stream there were hundreds of tandem pairs ovipositing. This photograph was taken with a wide angle lens by wading out into the water.

"Visited the River Ouse at Kempston Church End where high numbers of White-legged Damselfly were observed competing for oviposition sites. Flower heads of Yellow Water-lily appeared to be favoured and I observed up to 6 tandem pairs on one flower head. Repeatedly, tandem pairs would try to land on the flower and could not find a place. The flowers provide an ideal perch with the males adopting a 'sentinel' position whilst the females probed the underside of the flower with their ovipositors."

(Extract from author's field notes)

► Oviposition takes place in tandem either singly or in groups (right). The female sometimes submerges with the male guarding her in the sentinel posture.

survey during the early 1980s it was recorded along the Ouse from only two tetrads[10]. Similarly it disappeared from its main haunts along the River Ouzel. Despite a number of searches no records were obtained from the area until 1990 when small numbers were discovered between Slapton and Grove. At this time it was still absent from the river in Leighton Buzzard and Old Linslade.

Numbers have recovered and currently it can be the most numerous species present along suitable stretches of river. Wherever it occurs its distribution can be very patchy. This disjunct pattern appears to be due to differences in bankside vegetation. Emergent plants such as Reed Sweet-

grass are especially favoured. Other species such as Common Club-rush and Bur-reed appear to be avoided.

During the early 1990s it started to colonise the River Ivel from the River Great Ouse with the first records at South Mills in 1992. By 1996 it had moved down the Ivel and had reached the River Flit at Chicksands Base.

During July 2002 high numbers were discovered at the lake at Sundon Chalk Quarry. Many tandem pairs were observed ovipositing into floating stems of Fringed Water-lily. These observations were especially interesting as the species had rarely been encountered on stillwater sites in the county. The origins of this colony are unknown. The site is well visited and recorded and they were not present in 2000. Possible explanations include range expansion along the River Flit that rises nearby, although none have been seen along this stretch of the river. The nearest colony on the Flit is near to Chicksands, which is 15km away. The species has now been recorded at other stillwater sites and is breeding on the main lakes in Wrest Park. At Felmersham gravel pits egg laying has been observed in some years but follow up visits in subsequent years have failed to find any success of breeding.

Conservation status

A proven breeding species in Bedfordshire. It has often been quoted

to be susceptible to pollution but it is more likely to be affected by bank clearance operations[11].

Field notes

The conspicuously laterally flattened legs of the males which dangle below the body when in flight are used to display to females. During tandem formation and copulation the male is thought to use the legs to 'stroke' the female and to stimulate her to mate. Copulation typically takes between 13-27 minutes.

Both males and females undergo age related colour changes and develop progressively bolder black markings on the abdomen. Newly emerged specimens have an orangey-pink colouration. Immature *lactea* females are creamy-white with reduced markings and appear very pale. This phase develops into a light green mature phase with bolder markings along the dorsal surface of the abdomen. Once familiar with this species it is unlikely to be confused with anything else.

Eggs are laid in tandem with the female often submerging below the water's surface. This species exhibits group oviposition behaviour where numbers of tandem pairs are atttracted by each other to congregate at 'good' sites. Group ovipositing into floating leaves involving over 100 tandem pairs has been observed at suitable sites on the River Great Ouse and its backwaters.

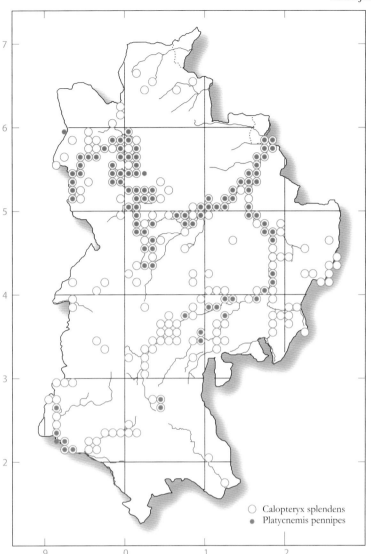

○ Calopteryx splendens
● Platycnemis pennipes

Flight period

In Bedfordshire the flight period is mid to late May to early September.

First date   13th May
Last date   9th September

Coincidence of White-legged Damselfly and Banded Demoiselle

A comparison of the distribution of the two species (above) shows a patchy distribution of the White-legged Damselfly (especially away from the River Great Ouse) resulting from its more selective habitat requirements.

"The evaluation of river quality data for Bedfordshire did not provide an explanation for differences in the distribution of P .pennipes and C. splendens. ....there is little evidence to support the view that this species is more susceptible to pollution than other species. It would appear to be more influenced by the habitat and nature of the vegetation. Populations in Britain have recovered over the last decade and when suitable conditions exist it is quick to colonize from nearby colonies and can sometimes be the most abundant species of Odonata."

(Extract from Cham 2003b[11])

References
[1] Palmer (1947)
[2] B. Verdcourt (pers.com.)
[3] K.E.West (1958)
[4] Palmer (1942-53)
[5] B.Lloyd (1944)
[6] S.Lloyd (1953)
[7] Hodgson (1959)
[8] Shepperson (pers.com.)
[9] Dawson (1980)
[10] Rowe, (unpublished report)
[11] Cham (2003b)

Large Red Damselfly   *Pyrrhosoma nymphula*

(Sulzer 1776)   **Family:** *Coenagrionidae*

▲ Male Large Red Damselfly attempting to mate with a female. The male has grabbed the thorax of the female and is attempting to form a tandem, using its anal appendages. The female is resisting the male's advances having just caught an Alder Fly which it is starting to consume.

▶ Large Red Damselflies ovipositing in tandem. The female is almost completely submerged, with the male still in tandem as a means of 'contact guarding' her from the attentions of other males.

Distinctive features

The Large Red Damselfly is the only red damselfly to occur in Bedfordshire. Both sexes are red with varying degrees of black markings. Males are predominantly red with red eyes and two red stripes on a bronze black thorax. Females occur in three colour forms, which vary in the amount of black on the abdomen.

It can be distinguished from the Small Red Damselfly *Ceriagrion tenellum*, a rare species of bogs and fens, which has red legs. The latter has never been recorded in the county.

Favoured habitat

Occurs throughout the British Isles and is found in a wide range of habitats. Appears to have a preference for well vegetated still water habitats such as ponds, lakes and canals, but occasionally occurs on rivers and ditches.

Bedfordshire: past and present

Although this is one of the most widely distributed species in the British Isles it has never been common in Bedfordshire. *"Generally distributed, but always in small numbers"*[1], *"At Ravensden, Flitwick Moor, Southill, Leighton Buzzard district"*[2], *"Recorded at a pond beside lane from top of Sunderland's Hill to Ravensden. It must be more common than records suggest"*[3], *"not recorded"*[4]. It was also comparatively scarce and local in north Hertfordshire in 1925 where small numbers were recorded at Knebworth Park[5].

Although still not common, it has in recent years colonised some of the Marston Vale brick pits as they have become mature. The largest population recorded in the county is at the north end of Coronation Pit where its numbers reach thousands in most recent years. This is exceptional, as rarely is it recorded in double figures elsewhere. Following the opening up of several small pools at Flitwick Moor during 2000 a small colony developed.

Conservation status

A proven breeding species in the county. Nationally it has shown some decline in intensively cultivated areas of eastern England.

Field notes

Males are very territorial, which may

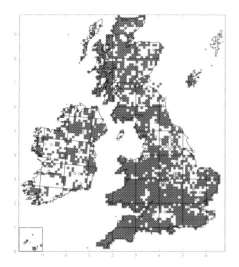

explain why many colonies comprise small numbers as they disperse. Copulation lasts for approximately fifteen minutes.

Males and females oviposit in tandem with the female often submerging. Eggs are laid into tissues of submerged plants or the underside of floating leaves.

Larvae live amongst roots and bottom debris and usually take one year to develop. The larvae are stout and have a characteristic dark X on the broad caudal lamellae. They are vigorously territorial. Midge larvae feature in their diet.

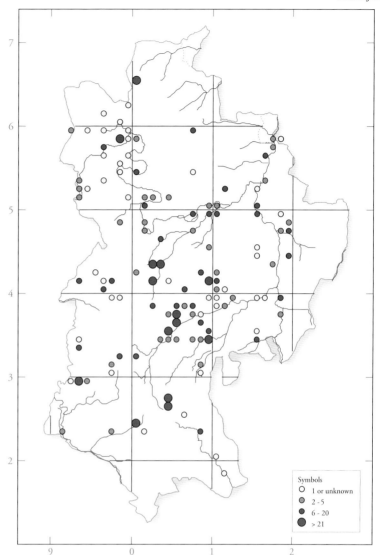

Symbols
○ 1 or unknown
◔ 2 - 5
● 6 - 20
⬤ > 21

Flight period

It is usually the first species on the wing with a highly synchronised emergence. They typically emerge from the second half of April through into May. In some years a warm, sunny spell in the middle of April can induce an earlier emergence of a few precocious individuals. Adults are on the wing usually until late July but are generally less visible later on in the flight period. In exceptional years it has been recorded as late as early September.

First date	17th April
Last date	3rd September

References
[1] B. Verdcourt (quoted by Palmer)
[2] Palmer (1947)
[3] K.E. West (1958)
[4] Longfield (1937)
[5] Hine (1934)

◄ Female Large Red Damselfly emerging in the early morning light at Coronation Pit, May 2000. The exuvia is still attached to the stem.

Blue-tailed Damselfly

(Vander Linden 1823)

Ischnura elegans

Family: *Coenagrionidae*

▲ A pair of Blue-tailed Damselflies in-cop. The female is of the male-like andromorph form. Flitton Moor, June 1997.

Distinctive features

Both males and females of the Blue-tailed Damselfly have the typical 'blue-tail' appearance. They have a black abdomen with segment S8 all blue and S9 black.

Females occur in a number of colour forms, which can lead to some confusion with identification (see below). They can either be immature or fully mature and current field guides should be consulted to distinguish them.

The Scarce Blue-tailed Damselfly is very similar. It is restricted to specialised microhabitat conditions and occurs at only one site in the county.

Favoured habitat

This is one of the commonest species in Britain. It is very common and widespread in Bedfordshire and is found along rivers and canals as well as most still water habitats. It will often be the only species present at sub-optimal habitat and is thought to be able to withstand mild pollution.

Bedfordshire: past and present

The Blue-tailed Damselfly is the commonest and most widespread species in Bedfordshire. There are more records for this than any other species in the county (appendix 4). This is the same situation as in Palmer's day[1]. In the 1940s it was reported as particularly abundant at Stevington and Oakley [2] and all along the Ouse [3].

Hine[4] records it as not uncommon in suitable localities in Hertfordshire. It was the "*Commonest damselfly in Bedford*"[5].

Conservation status

A very common species, which currently is not under any threat or even likely to be.

Field notes

This is often the only species active on dull days. On warm summer evenings activity can continue until

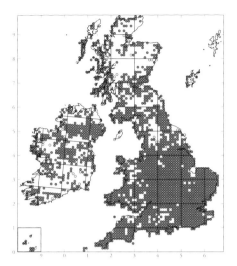

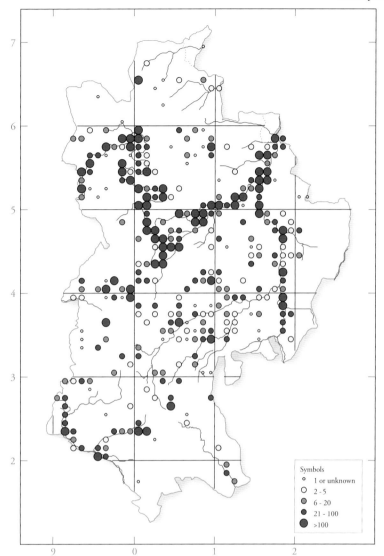

sunset. Females often oviposit at this time. They usually oviposit singly.

This species has been observed by the author and others[6] taking insect prey from spiders' webs.

"*At a small pond on the edge of Cranfield wood, near Roxton I was watching the flight of a female of the variety* rufescens-obseleta, *manoeuvring in between grass stems. It suddenly made a dash for a small black fly that was caught, but still alive and moving in a spider's web hanging from the flower spike of a* Calamagrostis *grass. She was able to capture it and fly away from the web without getting entangled. It was a rather risky manoeuvre but demonstrated the agility of dragonfly flight.*"

(Extract from author's field notes 25th August 1991)

In southern England it has a one-year life cycle. Maturation is reported to be rapid compared to other species. Exceptionally long copulation times have been recorded for this species. In Bedfordshire, times in excess of 1 hour

30 minutes have been noted, although times between 3-6 hours have been recorded elsewhere.

Flight period

In Bedfordshire it has a very long flight period and usually starts to emerge in early May remaining on the wing until end of September.

First date   2nd May
Last date   8th October

◄ Females occur in different colour forms that require careful identification.

♀ form *rufescens* (opposite top left) and

♀ form *violacea* (opposite bottom left) both showing the characteristic blue 'tail'.

♀ form *rufescens-obsoleta* (left) showing the brown 'tail'.

Symbols

○ 1 or unknown
○ 2 - 5
◔ 6 - 20
● 21 - 100
● >100

References

[1] Palmer (1947)

[2] B.B.West (in lit)

[3] D.W.Snow (in lit)

[4] Hine (1934)

[5] K.E.West (1958)

[6] M.Parr (in lit)

Scarce Blue-tailed Damselfly *Ischnura pumilio*

(Charpentier 1825)

Family: *Coenagrionidae*

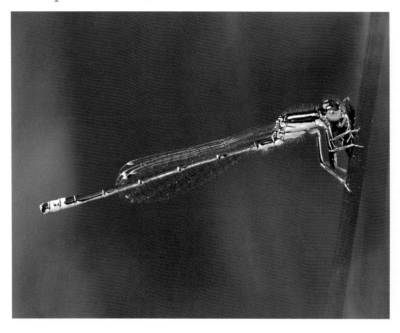

Distinctive features

Males have the typical 'blue-tail' appearance of Blue-tailed Damselflies. The markings on the thorax of males develop through green and turquoise to deep blue in mature individuals.

Females exhibit one of the most dramatic colour transitions during the maturation period. Immature females of the *aurantiaca* phase are bright orange. This phase lasts for 5-12 days before the orange coloration is gradually replaced by light greeny-brown in the mature female[1]. The abdomen is dorsally black throughout maturation and in very old females the thorax becomes dark brown almost black whilst the abdomen thickens as it becomes swollen with eggs.

▲ Male Scarce Blue-tailed Damselfly feeding on small micro moth at Sundon Chalk Quarry SSSI July 2002.

"Whilst conducting survey work in a large chalk quarry complex at Sundon in July 1987, I was surprised to observe a number of specimens of Ischnura pumilio *flying low over a wet seepage zone in the base of one of the quarries. I was familiar with the species from West Wales and did not immediately appreciate the significance of my find......*
...On impulse I looked for similar habitat at Houghton Regis Chalk pit. I.pumilio was located within 30minutes of arriving at the site!"

(Extract from John Comont's discovery in Bedfordshire[2])

▶ A female of the bright orange *aurantiaca* phase. Sundon Chalk Quarry SSSI, June 1992.

Favoured habitat

The Scarce Blue-tailed Damselfly occurs at scattered sites across southern Britain and Ireland where it has very specific habitat requirements. In western Britain and Ireland where the species is well established, it occurs in natural wetlands such as shallow bog pools and seepages in valley mires. In recent decades it has been reported increasingly from artificial wetlands such as those created by mineral extraction, newly created ponds and ditches. The creation of these man-made sites has provided an opportunity for colonisation of sites previously unavailable. It has a strong preference for shallow water conditions with little vegetation. A common feature of most sites is a degree of habitat disturbance, which perpetuates bare substrates, and openness of vegetation. Colonies at some of the new sites tend to be more transient and are more likely to be associated with the early stages of plant seral succession. At man-made sites it occurs at spring-fed seepages and shallow pools in areas of active workings. Water-filled vehicle

tracks also provide suitable microhabitat at such sites. Grazing and trampling by livestock maintain conditions at some sites. Colonies appear to undergo considerable fluctuations as habitat conditions change and it will eventually disappear from sites in which seral succession is allowed to proceed and dense vegetation develop.

The Scarce Blue-tailed Damselfly is primarily a Mediterranean species, being on the northern limit of its range in the British Isles. Water temperature throughout the year may be an important factor influencing its distribution. During the summer period the shallow water habitat at

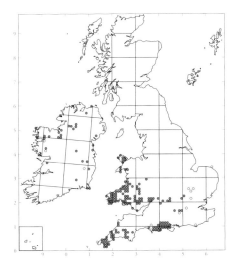

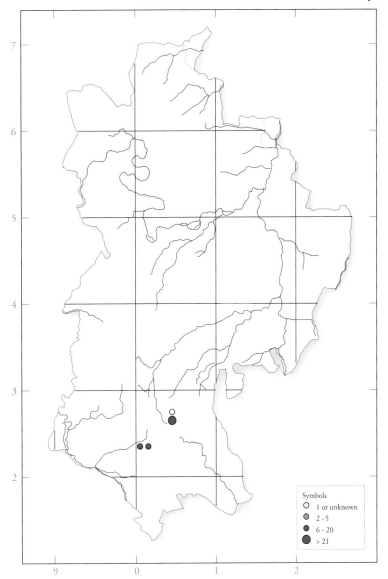

the Bedfordshire sites warms quickly. During the winter the continually seeping water from the springs also prevents freezing.

"*Visited Sundon Quarry today (14th February 1991). Last night was very cold with freezing fog and hoar frost, following on from a week of snow, which was covering the ground to a depth of three to four inches. Despite the sub-zero temperatures the spring lines were snow and ice-free where the water seeps out. The water in the runnels was not frozen even under several inches of ice and snow.*"

(Extract from author's field notes)

Bedfordshire: past and present

This species is currently restricted to just one small seepage area at Sundon Chalk Quarry. In recent years it was also recorded from similar habitat at Houghton Regis Chalk Quarry. The remaining site is the only colony in the region and is under threat.

Its discovery in 1987 in Bedfordshire at Sundon and Houghton Regis chalk pits came as a great surprise. These 'new' sites were some distance from the nearest known colonies in Britain and considered to be in atypical habitat. In neighbouring Buckinghamshire it was also recorded at similar habitat at College Lake NR in the same year. These discoveries were significant at the time and revised our understanding of the natural history of this species. However, further revelations were to come to light as a

result of the discovery. During her time as county recorder for Bedfordshire, Nancy Dawson had kept meticulous field notes of her observations. On the 1st July 1975 she had observed an unusual damselfly at Houghton Regis Chalk Quarry, which she believed to be Scarce Blue-tailed Damselfly. She made a detailed drawing of a female to which she made annotated notes. Excited by her find she wrote to the Biological Records Centre claiming to have found the species at the chalk quarry site. The reply was somewhat disappointing dismissing the record by stating-

"*a chalk quarry is the last place one*

▲ Map shows records from Houghton Regis where it was recorded up to 1999. The largest and only remaining colony is at Sundon Chalk Quarry SSSI.

county boundary. This was a site where the Natterjack Toad *Bufo calamita* was recorded in 'considerable abundance'[3]. In this area sand overlay clay forming shallow water pools that provided suitable conditions for spawning toads and damselflies.

Conservation status

Bedfordshire's rarest and most threatened species. The one remaining colony is very vulnerable to habitat loss from succession of vegetation around the seepage areas. Its numbers have been steadily decreasing over the last decade. The future of the Bedfordshire sites is uncertain. At the time of writing it already appears that it has been lost from Houghton Regis Chalk Quarry. Whilst both are designated as SSSIs the land adjacent to both sites is the subject of various applications for development.

Without human intervention the breeding sites will quickly disappear with the encroachment of vegetation. Ironically, the unauthorised activities of motorbikes and four-wheel drive vehicles have been instrumental in maintaining open areas of water at both sites, in the absence of more traditional conservation measures. These shallow seepage pools and runnels are an

▲▲ Sundon Quarry, August 1990, looking north. There is limited growth of vegetation in the seepage areas, due to the activities of off-road vehicles. High numbers were recorded at this time.

▲ A similar view in August 2002 showing vegetation with lush growth encroaching on the seepage areas. Numbers of Scarce Blue-tailed Damselfly have become much lower in these habitat conditions.

▶ Nancy Dawson's drawing of an *aurantiaca* female, along with notes made in 1975 at Houghton Regis Chalk Quarry. This was 13 years before its 'official' discovery.

would find Ischnura pumilio".
At this time it was thought to be a species of boggy habitat, with the nearest known sites in the New Forest, Hampshire.

Nancy's drawing clearly showed all the distinctive features of an immature *aurantiaca* phase female. She also noted it as common, with one being seen in copula. It seems remarkable that a species should go unnoticed for thirteen years. Even today, those visiting the Bedfordshire site for the first time are surprised that this species occurs in what, at first sight seems to be habitat where one would not expect to find dragonflies.

There is also an old record in 1824 from Gamlingay Heath, Cambridgeshire near the Bedfordshire

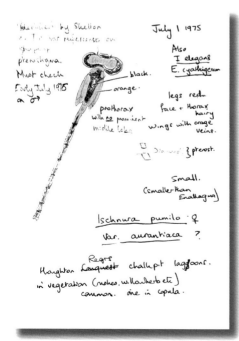

exceptionally rare and overlooked habitat in central southern England. Houghton Regis quarry became very dry during the mid 1990s becoming totally dry during the summer of 1997. Sundon Springs quarry remained wet during the same period but the encroachment of vegetation resulted in further shading of the seepage areas making them less 'attractive'.

Field notes

Females oviposit into emergent soft-stemmed aquatic plants in shallow water. Most favoured at Sundon are Rushes and Spike-rushes [4]. The female's abdomen is curved strongly enabling the ovipositor to be thrust into the plant tissue. Egg-laying commences just above water level and as each egg is laid the female descends into the water until the effects of surface tension on the thorax prevent it from entering any further. At this point the female either moves around the stem to repeat the procedure or flies off to find another stem. In the very shallow water of the seepage areas females will often lay into a stem right down into the chalky substrate. In these circumstances a white chalky deposit dries on the abdomen and wings when they have finished egg-laying and provides a useful means of determining which females have laid eggs.

The incubation time of eggs is difficult to observe under natural conditions but synchronised hatching after 17 days in eggs collected at Sundon has been observed under controlled conditions[5]. The larvae develop rapidly in the shallow water conditions and are generally found in or on silty, muddy substrates colonised by plants in the early stages of colonisation[6]. Larvae develop through several instars over the winter period accelerating development in the spring ready for emergence.

Although one gets the impression of a small weak-flying insect with a somewhat jerky flight the Scarce Blue-tailed Damselfly is highly dispersive.

Adults of both sexes and different age classes have been observed to fly vertically upwards until they are lost from sight[7]. This dispersal flight enables them to utilise rising thermals to reach higher levels where prevailing winds can carry them away to form new colonies elsewhere.

Flight period

In Bedfordshire the emergence period begins in late May in favourable years and continues through to end of July with a peak in mid-June.

First date   25th May
Last date   14th August

▲ Female ovipositing in shallow water in the seepage area at Sundon Chalk Quarry. Note the chalky substrate and lack of plant growth.

References
[1] Cham (1990b), Cham (1993)
[2] Comont (1988)
[3] Palmer (1948)
[4] Cham (1992)
[5] Cham (1992)
[6] Cham (1991), Cham (1993)
[7] Fox (1989), Cham (1993)

▼ Male in typical habitat at Sundon Chalk Quarry, July 1992. Photographed late one evening as the sun was going down.

Common Blue Damselfly *Enallagma cyathigerum*

(Charpentier 1840) Family: *Coenagrionidae*

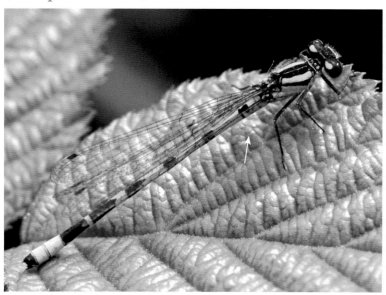

Distinctive features

The Common Blue Damselfly is one of several small blue damselflies that are superficially similar. The shape of the marking on the dorsal surface of abdominal segment S2 of males is distinctive, resembling a 'lollipop'. Females occur in three colour forms and are less easy to distinguish from other 'blues'. They require close examination of the markings on the side of the thorax. The Common Blue Damselfly lacks two dark lines that are present on the Variable and Azure Damselflies, with which it can be confused.

▲ Male Common Blue Damselfly clearly showing the characteristic 'lollipop' marking on segment two. Wyboston, July 2000.

▼ Common Blue Damselflies emerge in such high numbers that supports are often at a premium. Warren Villas NR 2003.

Favoured habitat

The Common Blue Damselfly favours open water habitat, such as can be found at large ponds, lakes, canals and rivers. The presence of underwater vegetation is key to this species. It is especially abundant on the flooded brick pits in the Marston Vale and flooded gravel pits along the Ivel and Ouse valleys. It reaches very high densities on open pits and lakes and its numbers will frequently outnumber any other species present at such sites.

Bedfordshire: past and present

A very common and widespread species throughout Bedfordshire and Great Britain. It has always been a common species in the county and lives up to its common name. Past records suggest that its abundance relative to the Azure Damselfly appears to have reversed in recent years.

"Fairly common and sometimes abundant locally, but less so than C.puella.*"[1]* *"Common on Flitwick Moor, Great Barford and Roxton. Abundant in many places in the south, generally distributed in the north."* [2]

Despite its abundance it has shown some decline or lost from some sites such as Flitwick Moor where open water has disappeared through vegetational succession.

Past records for Hertfordshire also indicate that it has always been common[3].

Conservation status

A proven breeding species that is very common and widespread in Bedfordshire and in no need of special conservation attention.

Field notes

The Common Blue Damselfly can be so common in some areas that observers tend to overlook many aspects of its behaviour. Careful observation of the breeding behaviour can reveal many hidden aspects of the natural history of this species. Males fly low and purposefully over apparently open water. In favourable years they can form vast swarms over apparently open water. These swarms tend to form where underwater plants occur just below the surface. Males hover over such areas waiting for females to resurface after ovipositing. They will also settle in tiers

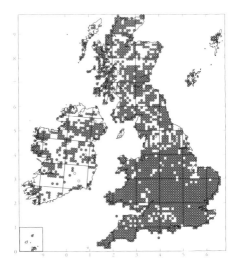

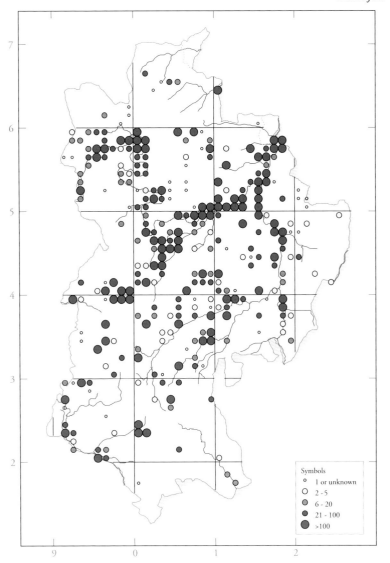

on nearby emergent stems with bodies held horizontally.

Copulation is usually away from water due to intense competition at the breeding sites. Males accompany females to water to oviposit. The tandem pair can be seen flying over open water looking for areas of underwater plants that just break the surface. As they settle the female is released and she starts to climb down to start ovipositing. She can remain underwater for more than 30 minutes and then finally floats to the surface. In most cases she is quickly retrieved by the males, which have been perched nearby. Where density is very high there can be much aggression between individuals and tandem males will sometimes submerge along with the female. Many males can often be observed hovering over prime sites where females have submerged to oviposit. An account of this behaviour at Rookery Clay Pit, before it was reworked, is worth recalling:

"*Tandem pairs approaching the prime ovipositing sites would immediately come under harassment from single males. The females in tandem appear from the video recordings to be the passive party in site selection. The males 'steer' the tandem in an attempt to avoid the attentions of other males. As the pair approach the water the female will readily grasp any plant that breaks the surface. Single males repeatedly harass the tandem pair*

trying to grasp the female with their legs. This would most often occur when the female was on or close to the water's surface. However, several observations were made of single males attempting this whilst the tandem was still in flight. In one tandem pair the male remained in tandem whilst the female started ovipositing just below the water surface. He remained attached for 43 seconds before releasing her to continue on her own. This contact guarding behaviour is perhaps understandable in light of the following observation.

A tandem pair was observed approaching the water with the male steering towards the patch where submerged vegetation just reached the surface. On contact with the water the female immediately submerged with the male still in tandem. The male released its hold

References

[1] Palmer (1947)

[2] B.Verdcourt (quoted by Palmer 1947)

[3] Hine (1934)

[4] Cham (2002c)

▲ Male Common Blue Damselflies 'swarming' over surface vegetation at prime oviposition site. They are waiting for females to float to the surface as they finish ovipositing underwater. Broom Gravel Pits July 2003.

▼ Common Blue males form 'tiers' as they rest on emergent stems waiting the arrival of females and tandem pairs. Broom Gravel Pits 2003.

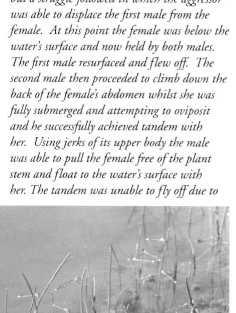

on the female just at the point at which his upper thorax was submerged. At this point a single male flew in and attempted to grasp the almost submerged female with its legs. The first male reattempted tandem with the female but a struggle followed in which the aggressor was able to displace the first male from the female. At this point the female was below the water's surface and now held by both males. The first male resurfaced and flew off. The second male then proceeded to climb down the back of the female's abdomen whilst she was fully submerged and attempting to oviposit and he successfully achieved tandem with her. Using jerks of its upper body the male was able to pull the female free of the plant stem and float to the water's surface with her. The tandem was unable to fly off due to

water logging of body and wings but the male managed to drag her to the nearest emergent stem about 0.3m away. After a few attempts they flew off in tandem."

(Extract from author's field notes[4])

If females are disturbed whilst ovipositing underwater they immediately become still and point their abdomen upwards trying to be as cryptic as possible. In very windy conditions it can be difficult for males to recover the females as they float up to the surface. On several occasions numerous dead and dying individuals have been found along the bank margins. There was an especially high mortality by this means at Elstow Clay Pit in 1990 when hundreds of females were found dead and dying along the windward margins.

Larvae can be found among submerged water plants as well amongst bottom substrates. Emergence often occurs in such high numbers that larvae take up every available emergence support. At Lidlington on 14th July 1989 every available stem rising from the water along the south-facing shore had a number of larvae and exuviae on it. At Warren Villas nature reserve during July 2002 and 2003 a similar mass emergence, numbering thousands of individuals, occurred during a period of warm weather immediately following cooler conditions.

"Exuviae and emerging adults were seen on almost every emergent stem in the favoured areas around the lake. Exuviae were on top of earlier emergences, sometimes building up three deep. Floating mats of filamentous algae were covered in tens of exuviae wherever they projected sufficiently high above the water's surface to allow a successful emergence."

(Extract from author's field notes 2002)

Flight period

In Bedfordshire it has a long flight period, being recorded from mid May to early October.

First date   4th May
Last date   17th October

Variable Damselfly

(Vander Linden 1823)

Coenagrion pulchellum

Family: *Coenagrionidae*

Distinctive features

As the vernacular name suggests, this species can be highly variable. The U mark on the dorsal surface of segment two is usually stalked and heavy. The antehumeral stripes on the thorax are usually either broken or thin, sometimes resembling an exclamation mark when viewed from above. The hind margin of the prothorax is heavily lobed and lacks a continuous thin blue margin. Any field records for Variable Damselfly in Bedfordshire should be treated with caution and carefully examined for diagnostic characteristics. Other blue damselflies such as Common Blue Damselfly are also superficially similar.

Favoured habitat

In neighbouring counties it favours mature gravel pits with lush aquatic vegetation and surrounding meadows. Despite visibly similar habitat being present it is not clear why its range does not extend into Bedfordshire.

Bedfordshire: past and present

The Variable Damselfly has not been recorded in Bedfordshire since the 1940s. Even at this time it was regarded as a rare species. Currently it has a scattered distribution over parts of England and Wales and just extends its range into Scotland. It occurs in adjacent counties, Buckinghamshire (VC 24) and Huntingdonshire (VC31). In the latter it is found in high numbers at some of the River Great Ouse valley gravel pit sites at Huntingdon and St.Ives, where it is often the most abundant species.

It was described by Palmer[1] as: "*rare and local, but possibly overlooked in the county. One male and a female from the River Great Ouse at Biddenham 1941 and Stevington 1943*".

B.B.West[2] recorded an individual at Sharnbrook in 1948. One was recorded at Grovebury Pits, Leighton Buzzard and a form with the thorax lacking the blue shoulder stripes was taken at Bromham in 1947[3]. It was also listed for Bedfordshire by Adams[4] with Hine[5] recording occasional records for Hertfordshire. It is possible that this species could again appear in the county at some time.

Flight period

Mid May to beginning of August.

▲ Pair of Variable Damselflies 'in-cop', photographed at mature gravel pits near St.Ives (VC31).

References
[1] Palmer (1947)

[2] Palmer (1948)

[3] K.E.West (1958)

[4] Adams (1945)

[5] Hine (1934)

◄ Male Variable Damselfly feeding on small fly. This male has very reduced antehumeral stripes that look like an exclamation mark!

Azure Damselfly

(Linnaeus 1758)

Coenagrion puella

Family: *Coenagrionidae*

▲ Male Azure Damselfly showing the characteristic U marking on segment two. Note also, the two short stripes on the side of the thorax, that distinguish this species from Common Blue Damselfly. Wyboston, June 1997.

References

[1] Palmer (1947)

[2] K.E.West (1958)

[3] Hine (1934)

[4] Thompson (1997)

▶ Going, going, gone! Azure Damselfly larva feeding on a frog tadpole. It has caught the prey and is holding it firmly with the hooks on the front of its mask. This restrains the struggling prey while the mandibles set about the process of mastication and ingestion. As it digests its food the dark contents can be seen moving down the damselfly's gut.

Favoured habitat

Very common throughout Britain and Europe and one of the most widespread species in southern Britain. It is also common and widespread throughout Bedfordshire, mainly at ponds and small to medium sized lakes with submerged aquatic plants and plants with floating leaves, such as Broad-leaved Pondweed.

It favours well-vegetated, sheltered habitat compared to Common Blue Damselfly, which is to be found in more open habitat. It has been recorded along slow stretches of rivers and canals. It often breeds in garden ponds.

Bedfordshire: past and present

It has always been a common species in the county and surrounding area. *"Very common in most localities, frequenting both ponds and running water."*[1] *"Generally common."*[2]

In the past it was also one of the commonest species in Hertfordshire, sometimes occurring in great numbers[3].

Currently there are many sites in Bedfordshire where high numbers are recorded in most years. The lakes

Distinctive features

The Azure Damselfly is one of several 'blue' damselflies that can be confused with each other. Males are bright blue with black markings, with a U shape on the dorsal surface of segment 2 being a key characteristic. However, care should be taken as this can be variable and can cause confusion with Variable Damselfly. Females occur in green and blue forms and also exhibit variation, which again can be confused with Variable Damselfly as well as Common Blue Damselfly.

The two short stripes on the side of the thorax of both sexes distinguish it from the Common Blue Damselfly.

at Wrest Park have an exceptional population with numbers into thousands in good years.

Conservation status

A proven breeding species that is common and widespread in the county.

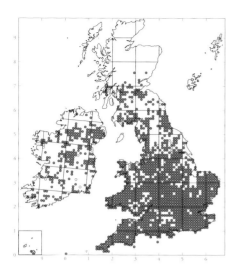

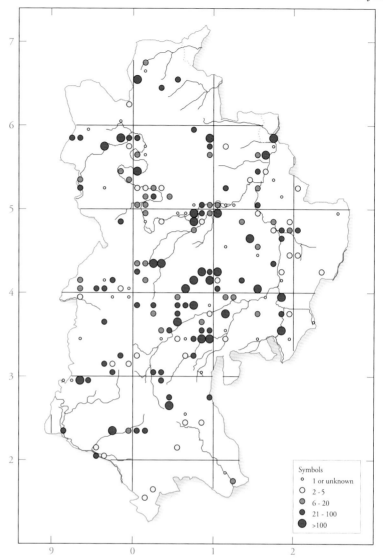

Field notes

Males are not territorial. They fly close to the water's surface and perch close to the top of vegetation. Copulation takes approximately 30 minutes. The eggs are laid into floating or submerged plants whilst the male and female remain in tandem. This can last for some 90 minutes.

In southern Britain it has a one year life cycle. Individuals can often be found feeding well away from water along hedge banks, field margins and woodland glades.

Larvae are found in living and dead vegetation where they actively hunt. They will tackle prey much larger than themselves and have been observed taking frog tadpoles. A female has been known to live for 26 days and produced 15 clutches of eggs (estimated at a total of 4,200 eggs)[4].

A single heavily marked male, resembling a Variable Damselfly, was recorded at Flitton Moor in June 1991. This demonstrates the need for careful examination of 'unusual' specimens to avoid misidentification and highlights the need to refer to a good field guide.

Flight period

In Bedfordshire emergence starts in early May with adults typically remaining on the wing until early September.

First date   1st May
Last date   17th October

▼ Female Azure Damselfly.

Red-eyed Damselfly

(Hansemann 1823)

Erythromma najas

Family: *Coenagrionidae*

▲ A male Red-eyed Damselfly 'guarding' a floating leaf of Broad-leaved Pondweed. This individual is also regulating its body temperature by orienting its body relative to the direction and angle of the sun. Wrest Park, July 2003.

Distinctive features

The Red-eyed Damselfly takes its name from the blood red eyes of the males, which are conspicuous even from a distance. Both sexes appear more robust than other damselflies, especially when the other species are present for comparison.

The male's abdominal segments 9 and 10 are blue. Females have brown-red eyes and lack the blue on the abdomen. Following the discovery of Small Red-eyed Damselfly in Bedfordshire, care needs to be taken to distinguish the two species.

Females are less distinctive with brown-red eyes and a lack of the blue 'tail'.

Favoured habitat

The Red-eyed Damselfly has a southern distribution in England and the Welsh borders, where it favours still water sites with expanses of floating vegetation. It also occurs along slow-flowing rivers and canals where the flow is slow enough to facilitate the growth of plants with floating leaves. Especially favoured are Yellow and White Water-lilies, Fringed Water-lily, Broad-leaved Pondweed, Amphibious Bistort leaves, Rigid Hornwort and floating mats of surface algae (blanket weed).

Bedfordshire: past and present

Bedfordshire records show that this species has become more abundant over the last two decades. This is also the case nationally where there appears to have been some range expansion westwards and northwards. In recent years there have been some colonies in the county that reach very high numbers. This is especially so at stillwater sites at Felmersham NR, Wyboston Lakes, Priory Country Park and Wrest Park,

where floating vegetation is abundant. The appearance of large floating mats of algae has led to colonisation of 'new' sites in the county, which would otherwise be unattractive to this species.

The map shows a distribution

▶ Mass emergence of Red-eyed Damselflies at Wyboston Lakes in June 2003. In one small area all flower heads of Amphibious Bistort were covered in exuviae and emerging adults.

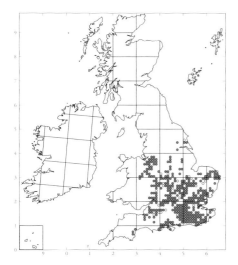

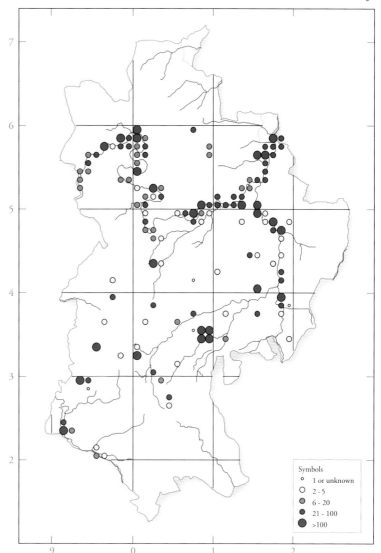

pattern in Bedfordshire associated with the River Great Ouse corridor with its numerous gravel pits. Elsewhere in the county it occurs on most of the main lakes where floating plants are abundant.

In the past it was reported as frequent along some parts of the Ouse (B.Verdcourt quoted by Palmer) especially at Bromham, Oakley, Stevington, Willington [1]. *"Fairly common on reach of River Ouse between Turvey and Newton Blossomville."* [2] It was common at Felmersham in the 1960s [3]. During an RSPB survey in the early 1980s it was recorded along the Ouse from, surprisingly, only two tetrads [4]. It was reported to be one of the commonest species on the Upper Ouse in June 1986 [5]. Interestingly there are no early records from the River Ivel. This is probably due to the lack of suitable habitat following extensive modification to this river.

Early records from Hertfordshire also suggest that this species was previously less common than it is today. Hine [6] recorded it as very local and only a recent addition to the Hertfordshire list. He took three specimens in June 1927 from the River Colne near Aldenham.

Conservation status

A proven breeding species in the county. Clearance operations or increased water velocity, which reduce the amount of floating vegetation, will have a negative impact on this species.

Field notes

Mature males spend long periods of time perched on floating leaves of lily pads and other floating vegetation, which they use as territorial platforms. The powerful but somewhat hovering flight is low over the water's surface, as they make sorties to capture prey or see off rival males. Several observers have noted that they are often 'buzz-bombed' by Common Blue Damselflies and forced to move away from the lake margins to avoid competition [7]. This does not appear to be the case at Bedfordshire sites where the species can

▲ A tandem pair of Red-eyed Damselflies ovipositing into Rigid Hornwort. The female is submerging to oviposit accompanied by the male. Note the dip in the water's meniscus as she does this. Wrest Park, July 2003.

▼ A tandem pair of Red-eyed Damselflies ovipositing underwater. Note how an envelope of air is trapped around their bodies. Wrest Park, July 2003.

hold its own against the other species. Males have been observed to feed over the water on Mayflies *Ephemera danica* and Caddis Flies.

Mating most often takes place over the water where tandem pairs settle on floating vegetation. Pairs usually remain in tandem during egg-laying which serves as an efficient mechanism for fending off other males. The eggs are usually laid into aquatic plants such as Rigid Hornwort or Water-milfoil or the undersides of floating vegetation;

especially lily pads and Amphibious Bistort. Tandem pairs will often descend more than 0.5 metres below the water's surface and in some cases have remained submerged for more than 30 minutes during oviposition. The female sometimes separates from the male continuing to oviposit underwater alone. On completion she releases her grip and floats to the surface assisted by the bubble of air entrapped between the wings and body.

When population densities are high there is a tendency towards group oviposition, which offers safety in numbers and indicates good sites (see photograph opposite).

"*now abundant in some quiet backwaters at Willington (partly in Renhold).....In one stretch which is covered with water lily leaves, over thirty were concentrated in comparative amity. The females join the all-male concentration, in our opinion, in the late afternoon, when egg laying takes place. The female is often totally submerged by the male and forced by him to lay her eggs quite a long way down stems and submerged leaves.*"

(K.E.West [8])

Larvae can be found amongst submerged vegetation of various types and can take 1-2 years to develop. The colour of larvae is variable, ranging from brown to green depending on the type of aquatic plants on which they are living. They have a distinctive robust appearance; the abdomen has a banded appearance and the characteristic caudal lamellae have dark banding with rounded tips. They are highly active and will readily use their large caudal lamellae to propel themselves through the water by means of rapid lateral movements of the abdomen.

Emergence takes place on submerged plants where they break the water's surface as well as on bankside vegetation. At some of the lakes at Wyboston, where they occur in high numbers, emerging adults and exuviae have been found covering the flowering spikes of Amphibious Bistort well away from the bank.

Flight period

In Bedfordshire emergence begins in early May in warm springs, with adult numbers reaching a peak in June and early July. This species appears to be extending its flight period and over the last five years it has been recorded well into September.

First date   3rd May
Last date   10th September

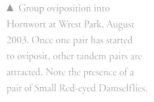

▲ Group oviposition into Hornwort at Wrest Park, August 2003. Once one pair has started to oviposit, other tandem pairs are attracted. Note the presence of a pair of Small Red-eyed Damselflies.

◄ The larvae have very distinctive caudal lamellae that are used as paddles to move through the water Felmersham, April 1993.

References
[1] Palmer (1947)
[2] K.E.West (1958)
[3] B.B.West (pers.com.)
[4] J. Rowe (unpublished report)
[5] Dawson (1987)
[6] Hine (1934)
[7] Benton (1980), Winsland (1983)
[8] K.E.West (1952)

Small Red-eyed Damselfly   *Erythromma viridulum*
(Charpentier 1840)   Family: *Coenagrionidae*

Distinctive features
The Small Red-eyed Damselfly takes its name from its red eyes. It can easily be confused with the slightly larger Red-eyed Damselfly. The eye colouration of males appears as a brighter 'tomato' red than the larger species. The blue on the abdomen is also more extensive, with the sides of segments 2 and 8 being blue in addition to 9 and 10. This is most noticeable when individuals are viewed from the side. The colour of the thorax in the females develops through green to blue with age. A field guide should be consulted wherever possible to confirm identity of this species.

▲ Tandem pair of Small Red-eyed Damselflies ovipositing into Rigid Hornwort at Wrest Park, August 2003. The male hovers in a sentinel posture to enable a rapid escape from predators.

▶▶ Group oviposition of Small Red-eyed Damselflies at Wrest Park, August 2003. One pair attracts others to start ovipositing.

▶ Mating pair of Small Red-eyed Damselflies on Water-lily pad at Priory Country Park, August 2003. The male is transferring sperm to his secondary genitalia prior to copulation.

Favoured habitat
The favoured habitat in Bedfordshire is mainly lakes and large ponds with an abundance of submerged vegetation. All sites have Rigid Hornwort, Water-milfoil or Canadian Waterweed as the prime plant species. These form dense patches that create a patterned mosaic on the water's surface, that attracts the species. The additional presence of floating leaves of Water-lilies appears to make a site more attractive. Other favoured plant species include Mare's-tail which has a similar appearance to its underwater leaves. The favoured habitats in Britain are mainly ponds, small lakes and farm reservoirs although it has also been recorded in narrow ditches in Essex and Kent.

Bedfordshire: past and present
The Small Red-eyed Damselfly is a recent colonist to Great Britain, having been discovered in Essex in July 1999 [1]. In subsequent years, further influxes from the continent occurred along the East Anglia coastal region

with increasing movement inland. In the summer of 2000 new colonies were discovered in Essex and the Isle of Wight [2]. It had been predicted that the species was likely to continue its range expansion in a similar fashion to the rapid colonisation of the Netherlands [3]. The summer of 2001 witnessed a significant immigration into the British Isles. The number of 'new' records from south-east England and the fluctuating numbers reported in early July through to September suggested that many individuals were

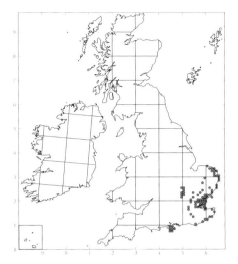

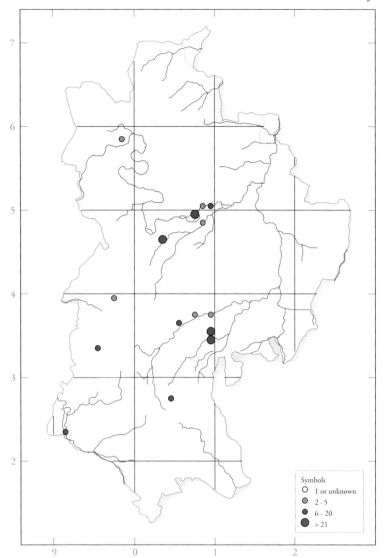

dispersing from continental Europe. This colonisation is the first of its kind as no other migrant damselfly species has established such widespread colonies in the British Isles.

During the 2001 influx it was discovered at Priory Country Park by Dave Ball and subsequently at Sundon Chalk Quarry by Lol Carman. These Bedfordshire records were significant at the time as they represented the most inland records and demonstrated the dispersal abilities of the species over a relatively short time period[4]. Follow-up visits at Priory Country Park during July 2002 revealed a number of adults including ovipositing pairs in exactly the same area of Hornwort where it had been discovered in the preceding year. This was suggestive that it has successfully bred during its first year in the county. During August 2002 it was recorded at Willington on a small pool with abundant submerged vegetation, a sand quarry at Linslade, two of the ponds at Wrest Park, a pond at Brogborough and one of the ponds on the Priory Business Park, Bedford. In each case the plant species were either Rigid Hornwort or Water-milfoil.

During June 2003 attempts were made to establish proof of breeding at Priory Country Park. The author accompanied Rosie Pallister using a boat to sample areas of Hornwort in the middle of the Finger Lakes. A number of larvae were found by searching through clumps of Hornwort, which were later identified as Small Red-eyed

▼ Small Red-eyed Damselflies can often be seen resting in areas where submerged plants break the water's surface. Here a male is seen in typical resting position on algae covering a patch of Rigid Hornwort.

Damselfly. This was the first time larvae had been recorded in Britain and was conclusive proof of successful breeding in Bedfordshire. During 2003 adults were recorded in high numbers on the lakes at Priory and Wrest Park. It was also recorded again at Brogborough, Linslade and Sundon as well as new sites at Clophill, Flitton, Kempston, Maulden and Woburn Park.

Conservation status

This is a recent migrant that has colonised much of south-east England in the first few years of the millennium. Its range is still expanding across Europe and Britain and is not in need of any immediate conservation attention. The presence of Hornwort is the single greatest factor if this species is to breed. Extensive 'weed' clearance will have a negative impact.

The discovery in Bedfordshire

"Arriving at Priory about 14:20 BST, and not being entirely sure what I was looking for, I first tried the dipping platform on the Visitor Centre side of the Finger Lakes, where I had seen Red-eyed Damselfly in the past. After a while I went round to the large spit which bisects the Finger Lakes, and looked at the first set of fisherman's steps on the left, looking north-west back towards the Visitor Centre. This looked much better, lots of emergent vegetation, lily pads and scum, and quite a few damselflies about. Within a few minutes I noticed Red-eyed Damselflies in flight, and followed one until it settled on a patch of scum to my left. Unfortunately it was facing almost directly away and was slightly against the light, but the features I could see seemed interesting. It seemed smaller and slenderer than the other Red-eyeds I had seen in flight, and to have more black at the extreme back end, though it was a little too far away to see the exact pattern. Also I could see little or no red in the eyes, looking from behind, though it obviously was a Red-eyed sp. This suggested duller eyes than *najas*, and together with the small size and slenderness and appearance of more black on segment ten suggested *viridulum*. However, I thought I had probably seen both species…. The next morning, Saturday 25th August, I had bought a telescope, and soon started to pick up Red-eyeds. After a few minutes I located a male sitting on a small patch of scum, facing left and exactly broadside on in brilliant light, about ten metres out. It had

a huge amount of blue under the rear end, with the division between black above and blue below sloping shallowly down and forwards. Fortunately there were male *najas* available for comparison which clearly showed the division between the black segment eight and blue segment nine as vertical …….. we had found a second Small Red-eyed male in view at the same time, a metre or two to the left of the first, another rather closer to us which could have been one of these which had moved, and also a female which two males tried to mate with in quick succession, and which was ignored by male Red-eyeds. ……These included (at least) a pair in cop and another male.

At all times, the easiest to see and most distinctive difference between male *najas* and *viridulum* was the pattern of blue on segments eight and nine. This seemed to be totally diagnostic, with little or no variation amongst the individuals of either species, which we saw. The blue wedge on the underside of segment eight on *viridulum* was amazingly obvious, even being visible from directly above as a narrow line of blue towards the rear of the segment. All *najas* had completely black eight and blue nine (except for a very narrow band of dull blue on the extreme underside of both segments, which was difficult to see, even from the side?) . This gave a vertical division between the black and blue as opposed to the very shallow sloping division on eight in *viridulum*, with only a thin slice of black on top of the segment. After the first day I forgot to check for the black on ten on *viridulum*, though this wasn't striking, nor was any difference in the amount of blue under segment one.

E.najas has a very distinctive jizz, to use a birding term, with the front of the insect looking very dark, bulky and almost bee-like compared to other smaller damselflies, whereas *viridulum* is much closer in size and build to say, Common Blue or even Blue-tailed. However, I thought that none of these other differences were safely diagnostic, as there was some variation in size in both species, and things like eye colour varied to some extent with light conditions. I also thought that *viridulum* approached the bank less often and less near than *najas*."

(Extract from Dave Ball's field notes August 2001)

Field notes

The Small Red-eyed Damselfly is a smaller damselfly than its close relation and can easily be overlooked. There is very little published information on its natural history in Britain due to its recent arrival. The original discovery in Bedfordshire by Dave Ball is worth recalling as it demonstrates some of the initial difficulties in determining the species.

Once the observer is familiar with the species the greater extent of blue on the abdomen is quite noticeable through binoculars. The female especially, has more blue than the females of Red-eyed Damselflies and when seen in tandem with males the blue predominates. Mating occurs on floating vegetation away from the bank. The males adopt an upright stance whilst in tandem curving the tip of their abdomen downwards in order to encourage the females to mate. Before copulation the male transfers sperm to the secondary genitalia whilst in tandem. Copulation is relatively short lasting between 5-10minutes. Oviposition takes place in tandem with the female usually ovipositing in Rigid Hornwort or Water-milfoil just reaching the water's surface. Unlike the Red-eyed Damselfly the Small Red-eyed Damselfly does not submerge below the water's surface during oviposition.

There is a marked tendency for the Small Red-eyed Damselfly to oviposit in groups[5]. This behaviour has been observed at Wrest Park and also Priory Country Park where on 27th July 2003 hundreds of tandem

pairs were observed ovipositing into Hornwort in a relatively small area. At Wrest Park tandem pairs of both species were ovipositing in the same areas of Hornwort. This communal behaviour provides them with a means to detect the small fish that predate them at this site. It also reduces the amount of time required to search for prime sites, thus increasing the amount of time available for egg-laying. At the Bedfordshire sites most ovipositing activity has been observed during the warmer sunny periods. During the cloudier periods they seem to disappear and at one English site have been found clinging to the branches of Willow. By recording group egg-laying behaviour it may be possible to gain a better insight into the size of the population at a site than observing individual adult males.

Flight period

Nationally the peak of the flight period for Small Red-eyed Damselfly is later than the Red-eyed Damselfly. In Bedfordshire it has been recorded on the wing from the first week of July to the first week of September, although nationally it has been recorded as early as June and later into September.

First date   6th July
Last date   4th September

▲ The larvae of Small Red-eyed Damselflies spend their underwater development hunting amongst the leaf whorls of Rigid Hornwort. This larva at Priory Country Park in June 2003 was the first definitive proof of breeding in the county. It was also the first time larvae had been found and photographed from any British site since its discovery in Essex in 1999.

References

[1] Dewick and Gerussi (2000)

[2] Cham (2001)

[3] Ketelaar (2000), Wasscher (1999)

[4] Cham (2003a)

[5] M.Elvidge (pers. com.)

◄ Rosie Pallister searching for Small Red-eyed Damselfly larvae as part of her study of the dragonflies of Priory Country Park. A boat was used to get out to the extensive areas of Rigid Hornwort in the middle of the Finger lakes.

Hairy Dragonfly

Brachytron pratense

(Müller 1764)

Family: *Aeshnidae*

▲ Hairy Dragonfly males (left) appear less robust than females (right). Priory CP, June 2000 and Wyboston, June 1999.

Distinctive features

The Hairy Dragonfly is a small hawker dragonfly. On close examination adults have a conspicuously hairy thorax. Males have two green shoulder stripes. When seen at rest the long thin pterostigma is a distinctive feature.

It is an early flying species with a relatively short flight season and is most likely to be encountered during May and June. For this reason it is unlikely to be mistaken for other hawker species that appear later. However, in exceptional cases it could be confused with the Southern and Migrant Hawker.

Favoured habitat

In Bedfordshire adults favour stillwater habitat with plenty of emergent vegetation. Males are usually encountered patrolling along the margins of tall emergent vegetation. They fly in and out of stands of Bulrush and Common Club-rush where females are likely to oviposit. Site selection by females appears to be determined by the presence of the floating decomposing stems of emergent plants. The species has also been recorded along linear habitats such as rivers and ditches.

Bedfordshire: past and present

The Hairy Dragonfly is a relatively recent colonist to Bedfordshire. In the mid to late 1990s it was undergoing a significant range expansion across southern Britain, being recorded in many new areas. Careful observation by John Comont led to the first confirmed county record during 1996 when a single male was observed patrolling around emergent vegetation at the margins of a small pond at Bromham Lake NR. Following this

discovery the author recorded several males and a female from Felmersham NR the following day. Furthermore, a single exuvia was found during this visit, which confirmed that breeding had already taken place in the county. Unknown at the time, Bernard Nau and Rosemary Brind had also recorded flying adults at Priory

▶ Hairy Dragonflies get their name from the hairs that fringe the thorax and abdomen.

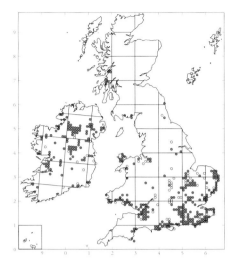

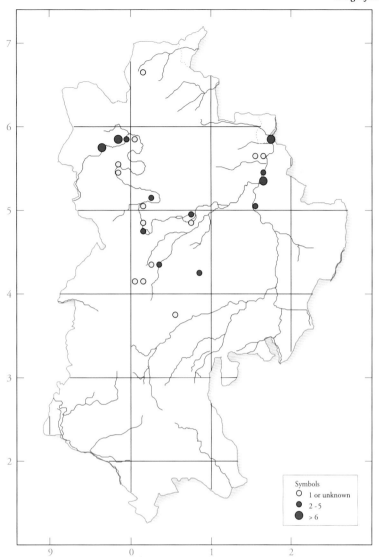

Park, Peter Almond had recorded it at Bromham Lake and Stewartby and Kevin Sharpe at Coronation Pit. Further observations at Felmersham over the rest of the season confirmed a female ovipositing into the dead floating stems of Common Club-rush at 8.00am one morning.

It is now well established as a breeding species in other counties in southern England and its range continues to expand. The discovery of the exuviae at Felmersham showed the species had been present in the county for at least two years (the life cycle is two years) prior to the first confirmed record. This added further weight to a sighting of a small hawker at Kempston Church End seen during June 1993, which could not be confirmed, but was most likely this species. It was also confirmed as breeding at Priory Park in 1998 when exuviae were found at the Finger Lakes. Further records during 1997-8 came from Begwary Brook NR, Bromham Lake NR, Coronation Pit and Girtford gravel pit lakes. Females were observed ovipositing into Common Club-rush stems at Coronation Pit during June 2002. The regular occurrence of males at this site suggests that it is now well established in the area. The current distribution in the county appears to be influenced by the River Great Ouse corridor and Marston Vale, which provide routes

for dispersal. During the early 2000s it had started to move down the Ivel valley.

In former times the species had a restricted range and was thought to be confined to the Broads, fens and coastal levels. There was an unconfirmed sighting in the county at Willington Staunch Pool in June 1957 by B.B.West -

"*In spite of repeated visits in 1958 to this location the species has not been seen since…. We have taken it plentifully in the past at Wicken Fen and on the Broads*".

Hine[1] refers to a record in the Hertfordshire VCH published in 1845. No details were

▲ Hairy Dragonfly larva 'hugging' an underwater rotting plant stem. This behaviour along with its cryptic colouration enable it to blend in with its background and avoid predation. Note the white-coloured colonies of the freshwater protozoan, *Vorticella*, growing on its body. This suggests that larvae lead a sedentary life style.

References
[1] Hine (1934)
[2] Palmer (1947)

▶ Two Hairy Dragonflies emerging on Yellow Iris at Felmersham NR, May 2002. Several more exuviae were found in close proximity.

association with bottom plant debris at the lake margins. When observed under captive conditions they appear well camouflaged against the underwater stems. Larvae move slowly yet deliberately close to the stem while in search of their prey.

On 16th June 1998 a female was observed ovipositing into dead floating stems on the Finger Lakes at Priory Country Park when it was seen to fly up, catch a male Azure Damselfly and then fly into a treetop to consume it.

Flight period

In Bedfordshire it is usually the first large dragonfly on the wing each year. In the county its flight period is the last week of April in warm springs to the end of June.

First date	30th April
Last date	26th June

given. It was also reported from Northamptonshire, Huntingdonshire and Cambridgeshire[2].

Conservation status

The species is a proven breeding species in the county. It is a species of high conservation value both in the British Isles and Europe. Over zealous 'cleaning up' operations should be avoided, especially the removal of the rotting floating stems of emergent plants.

Field notes

Females oviposit alone, into dead floating stems of emergent plants. The presence of ovipositing females can often be heard before a sighting is made. They fly in between tall vegetation as they search for floating stems. It is in these areas that males can often be seen searching for females. They exhibit remarkable flying skills as they manouvre between the stems.

Larvae play 'dead' when disturbed and can be difficult to find when caught in a net. They have often been found in association with stems of Bulrush. At Felmersham NR early instar larvae have also been found in

Common Hawker
(Linnaeus 1758)

Aeshna juncea
Family: *Aeshnidae*

Distinctive features

There are no recent records for the Common Hawker in Bedfordshire and any records for the county should be treated with caution.

Both the Migrant Hawker and Southern Hawker can be confused with the Common Hawker, leading to unconfirmed records for this species.

The yellow costa distinguishes it from the other species. The paired dorsal blue spots along the brown abdomen extend to segment 10 (see arrow on photograph) unlike Southern Hawker where they form bands on segments 9 and 10.

▲ Male Common Hawker photographed at Thursley, Surrey. The diagnostic yellow costa on the leading edge of the wings can be clearly seen and is characteristic of this species.

Favoured habitat

Nationally, the Common Hawker is found on the lowland heaths and northern uplands. Despite its vernacular name it should be regarded as an uncommon species in need of protection in south-east England, where it is restricted to lowland heath and bogs.

Bedfordshire: past and present

The 'common' name can be misleading as nowhere in southern Britain can it be regarded as particularly common and it is easily confused with other species. Furthermore, experiences from other counties suggest that many records for this species can be attributed to misidentification[1]. Past records for this species appear at a time when the Migrant Hawker was still relatively unknown, yet becoming established as a regular breeding species in Britain. It was also at a time when the Migrant Hawker still had the vernacular name of Scarce Hawker, possibly further confusing and influencing the perception of this species' abundance.

Palmer[2] reports three records for Bedfordshire: at Stevington, October 1942, Kempston, 1943 and Ouse, 1944. He states that he, personally, had "*not yet taken it in the county*". Palmer[3] also reports it from Flitwick Moor on 13th September and a garden in Bedford on 31st August. These records were not qualified in any way. Palmer's diary entry for 13th September 1948 states:

"*on Flitwick Moor watched a dragonfly thought to be* A.juncea, *by its very pronounced blue spots, but could not capture it.*"

In view of the similarity with other Hawker species it is surprising that no mention was made of the yellow costa, which is diagnostic. Adams[4] also listed it. None of the Bedfordshire records have been supported by a voucher specimen or a photograph and should therefore be regarded as unconfirmed.

Flight period

From July to September in southern Britain.

References

[1] Mendel (1992)

[2] Palmer (1947)

[3] Palmer (1948)

[4] Adams (1945)

Brown Hawker

(Linnaeus 1758)

Aeshna grandis

Family: *Aeshnidae*

Distinctive features

A large distinctive hawker dragonfly. It is difficult to confuse with any other species. Both males and females have a brown thorax and abdomen with brown wings. There are two very prominent yellow diagonal stripes on the side of the thorax.

It rests in vegetation and often the first indication of its presence is the rustling of wings as it takes to flight when disturbed.

Can often be seen in high numbers feeding over sheltered meadows near to water.

▲ Pair of Brown Hawkers 'in-cop'. Copulation usually takes place hanging from bushes. Felmersham NR, August 1998.

Favoured habitat

The Brown Hawker is widespread across the county and breeds readily in slow-flowing rivers and a range of stillwater habitats. Females are attracted by floating logs and submerged roots in which they oviposit. Sheltered meadows, adjacent to the breeding site, are important as feeding areas.

Bedfordshire: past and present

The Brown Hawker is currently a very common dragonfly throughout the county.

In the past it was described by Palmer[1] as "*fairly common, though less generally distributed than* A.cyanea." Thought to be "*most abundant along the Ouse*". Palmer also reported it from woodland well away from water. "*Plentiful along the Ouse*"[2]. Since Palmer's day it has become more frequent and widespread than *A.cyanea*. Early records state that it was not recorded in north Hertfordshire[3].

Conservation status

A common and widespread species with no requirement for special management. The provision of rotting wood by the waters edge will attract females to oviposit. It is the second most abundant dragonfly species after the Common Darter (see Appendix 4).

Field notes

It is a voracious predator often catching quite large prey. Nancy Dawson[4] reports a Small White butterfly was caught in flight and consumed whilst settled on grass stem. The wings were discarded. One was also observed to catch and eat a Small Tortoiseshell butterfly[5]. At Marston Thrift ponds a female Brown Hawker was observed catching an adult male Common Darter. After an initial struggle the Darter was eaten up to the thorax leaving the wings still attached (see earlier section on predation).

Females oviposit into floating or partially submerged rotten wood and roots. At favoured sites a number of females have been seen ovipositing together.

Adults can often be seen flying late into the evening in semi-darkness. They also appear early in the morning whilst

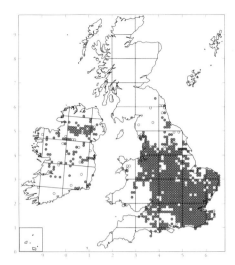

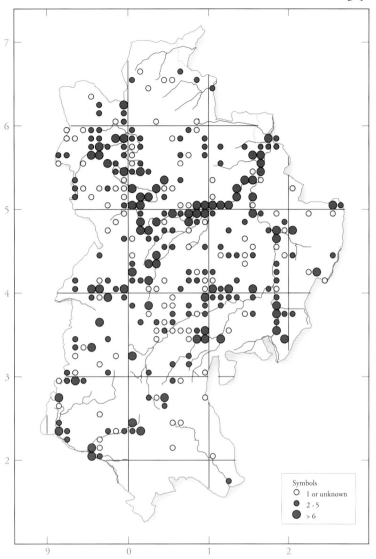

the air temperature is cool enough to keep other species at their roosts.

"On the 31st August 1986 we made an early morning visit to the River Great Ouse at Cardington Mill, Bedfordshire to look for roosting Odonata. The sun had already risen and was warming the bankside vegetation following a relatively cool night. At 07.20 our attention was drawn by the typical rustling of dragonfly wings coming from a dense patch of Common Nettles partially warmed by the sun.

Observation revealed a male Aeshna grandis flying between the nettle stems, its wings frequently making contact with the vegetation. Our initial impression was that it was trying to fly clear of the nettle patch having roosted there overnight. However, having flown clear several times it re-entered the nettles and continued to fly between the stems. It seemed rather puzzling that a dragonfly should risk damage to its wings by such unusual behaviour. Closer inspection revealed large numbers of chironomid midges roosting on the nettle leaves and these were being disturbed by the actions of the dragonfly as it flew between the nettle stems. At intervals the dragonfly would hover, catch and consume one of the midges before continuing this activity.

At this time in the morning there were very few prey insects on the wing and the nettle patch provided an ideal larder of food for the dragonfly. The midges were in rather inaccessible places on the nettle plants, such as the underside of leaves, and clearly this dragonfly was having great success in catching them, having once disturbed them. The dragonfly was observed feeding in this manner for nearly twenty minutes. Further along the riverbank two other A.grandis were observed in nettle patches exhibiting the same behaviour."

(extract from Cham and Banks[6])

Flight period

In Bedfordshire it has been recorded from the end of May in warm springs through to the last week of October.

First date   28th May
Last date   5th November

References

[1] Palmer (1947)

[2] West, K.E. (1957)

[3] Hine (1934), Lloyd, B. (1937)

[4] Dawson (1978)

[5] Dawson (1979)

[6] Cham and Banks (1986)

Southern Hawker

(Muller 1764)

Aeshna cyanea

Family: *Aeshnidae*

▲ Male Southern Hawker resting on Blackthorn during a warm afternoon at Willington Gravel Pits, September 2003. The two broad green stripes on the thorax are clearly visible.

Distinctive features

The Southern Hawker is one of the county's largest dragonflies. It has the appearance of being much greener than other hawkers due to the broad green thoracic stripes. Both sexes can appear similar but the male tends to have more blue markings on the abdomen. The blue markings on segments 9 and 10 (arrowed) form bands compared to the Common Hawker. It can be confused with the Migrant Hawker when seen in isolation but when seen together it is noticeably larger.

It can be seen flying late into the evening during warm periods. When flying in woodland it can sometimes appear very dark.

Favoured habitat

Both male and female Southern Hawkers will wander far and wide in search of new ponds and lakes. They favour any pool that has surrounding trees and bushes. It is also a frequent visitor to small ponds, especially garden ponds, where it will readily breed. Females search out mossy logs and stumps close to water, in which to oviposit. These can often be in shaded parts of a site. In shaded woodland pools this can sometimes be the only species that breeds. One of the best times of day to see Southern Hawkers is in the evening when they change their behaviour to feeding along woodland rides. Both Maulden and Chicksands Woods offer good opportunities to see them hawking for food as they space themselves out at intervals along the main rides.

Bedfordshire: past and present

Currently, it may not be as common in Bedfordshire as it used to be. Historical records show it to have been abundant across the county. Palmer[1]

records this *as "the commonest large dragonfly in the county"* a situation echoed for Hertfordshire[2,3]. *" very common in all southern counties." "Quite plentiful along the Ouse."*[5] In a review by K.E.West[6] it was noted as *"the commonest of the larger dragonflies particularly in the Ouse valley…..less plentiful in south of county."*

It is still a widespread breeding species in Bedfordshire occasionally seen in twos or threes but more often as single individuals. This is in contrast to Brown and Migrant Hawkers, which are often observed in double figure numbers.

▶ Male Southern Hawkers frequently visit garden ponds in search of females. They can appear inquisitive as they hover over likely areas. Author's garden pond, Silsoe, August 2002.

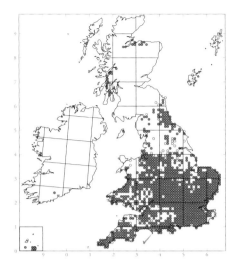

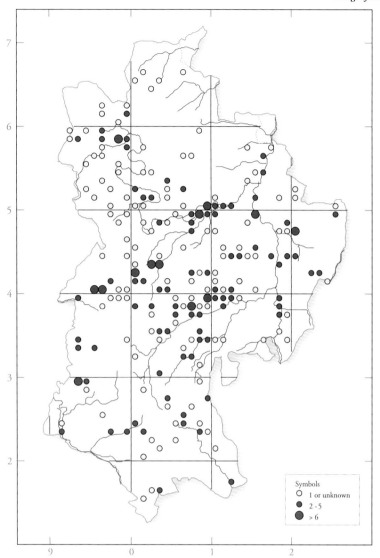

Conservation status

A species with no immediate needs for special attention. Garden 'wildlife' ponds are now one of the major habitat types for this species in eastern England. It can be attracted by leaving logs and rotting wood at the water's edge for females to oviposit.

Field notes

The males of this species often approach and hover very closely, appearing to be almost inquisitive. This is part of the male's search strategy whilst looking for females. They regularly visit ponds in search of females. Females oviposit alone in a range of places. Old mossy stumps in or near water are favoured but other more unusual substrates can be utilised. During one bout of egg-laying in August 2002 that lasted over an hour a female was observed egg-laying into a log and moss covered rocks more than a metre from water. Another more unusual observation at a garden pond involved the author as the substrate:

"At 16.00 hrs on 26th July 2001 it was a hot summer afternoon. A female A.cyanea visited my newly created garden pond in Silsoe (approx 4m diameter) searching around the margins for suitable oviposition sites. The pond was only 2 months old at this time and although some aquatic and emergent plants were present it probably offered sub-optimal habitat. There were no logs or other woody

substrate usually favoured by this species at the pond.

The pond appeared to be 'attractive' to the female although she circled it numerous times before settling on the grass lawn next to the pond. She was observed over a period of 70 minutes ovipositing at intervals for about 20 seconds into the turf before moving to search for the next suitable oviposition site. She settled on various plants around the pond for short periods of rest.

Aeshna cyanea is known to oviposit in 'unusual' places. There is a reference to egg-laying into a pair of training shoes while the person was still in them! This afternoon I was wearing shorts and I decided to experiment with my leg as potential substrate for the female to oviposit. To my surprise she settled

References

[1] Palmer (1947)

[2] Palmer (1930)

[3] Hine (1934)

[4] Longfield (1937)

[5] K.E.West (1957)

[6] K.E.West (1958)

[7] see appendix 2

▲ Female Southern Hawker ovipositing into moss growing on a log by the author's garden pond in Silsoe, August 2002.

▼ Southern Hawker larvae are voracious predators and will tackle prey as large as themselves. The mask is used to catch and restrain a Stickleback while the mandibles start ingesting it.

Although I have read of one attempt to oviposit into a dog's fur this is the first time I have heard of it attempting to oviposit into human skin." (extract from author's notes)

on my leg and attempted to oviposit in between the hairs on my leg and thigh. Her ovipositor was probing for suitable nooks and crannies in my skin but to no avail. This was attempted on two separate bouts. I experienced no unpleasant sensation and she quickly gave up and moved elsewhere. She also settled on my sheepskin slippers with further attempts to oviposit. These were also unsuitable and no eggs were laid. Following this she again resumed oviposition in the turf around the pond margins several cm's above the surface of the water.

Southern Hawkers are often encountered flying some distance from water in woodland. They will roost in hedgerows, gardens and along woodland rides. A male observed flying late one August evening in the author's garden eventually settled to roost in a holly/ivy hedge. It was hanging under a leafy twig that provided it with protection from the elements and potential avian predators. On another occasion in September a male roosted from 19.30 overnight hanging from a Holly leaf.

Both sexes have also been observed entering houses. One individual entered the author's house through an open patio door to fly through one room into another, only to get caught in net curtains. It was disentangled and released.

In order to monitor the number of individual females visiting a garden pond throughout a season, it is relatively easy to mark the wings of female Southern Hawkers when they come to oviposit. At the author's garden pond in Silsoe individuals were marked using small dots of paint on the forewings (see page 13). This can be applied using a fine camelhair brush[7]. Of eight that were uniquely marked, six were seen on further occasions returning to the pond. Other unmarked individuals were also seen on visiting the pond.

Larvae are frequently observed by owners of garden ponds as they crawl amongst the underwater plants. It is often a surprise to find how many subsequently emerge in the spring.

Flight period

In Bedfordshire the flight period is from the end of May in exceptional years through to end of October at the other extreme.

First date   18th May
Last date   2nd November

Hawker Dragonflies in Flight

One of the behavioural attributes that distinguishes dragonflies from other insect orders is their amazing agility and manouverability in flight. Such flight, combined with their high visual acuity, is required for catching prey (such as flying insects), seeing off rival males, as well as finding and connecting with potential mates.

Hawker Dragonflies in particular are often encountered flying at close range. The males of Southern Hawkers will appear inquisitive as they 'investigate' the human observer. Migrant Hawkers spend much of their time flying in and out of stands of emergent vegetation. These are all search strategies where the male is looking for females.

The study of dragonfly flight has been greatly enhanced by the availability of high speed filming techniques[1]. The equipment required can be very expensive and only in the realms of the professional filmaker. Modern video and still cameras however, can be used to record some aspects of flight in the field. Both film and digital still cameras fitted with fast motor drives and using fast shutter speeds offer opportunities to capture flight sequences, which can aid the study of flight behaviour. This is a technique that few people have tried.

The success rate can be low but patience is often rewarded. The flight sequence opposite shows a male Migrant Hawker hovering over marginal vegetation along the bankside at Priory Country Park. The changing positions of the wings enable the dragonfly to hover or gain thrust for forward movement. When hovering, wing movement known as 'counterstroking' is used by dragonflies[1]. One pair of wings is on the way up when the other are on their way down. The abdomen moves from side to side to stabilise the dragonfly in one position.

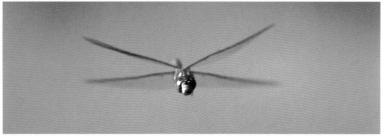

▲ Male Migrant Hawker in hovering flight at the Finger Lake, Priory CP, September 2003. Photographed at $^{1}/1000^{th}$ second using a rapid burst from the camera's motordrive.

Reference
[1] Rüppell, G. in Silsby, J. (2001)

Migrant Hawker
(Latreille 1805)

Aeshna mixta
Family: *Aeshnidae*

▲ Pair of Migrant Hawkers 'in-cop'. Felmersham, September 2003. The reduced antehumeral stripes are clearly shown on the male and almost absent on the female.

Distinctive features

The Migrant Hawker is superficially similar to both the Southern Hawker and Common Hawker. It is noticeably smaller, especially when seen together. Size can sometimes be difficult to determine when seen flying alone.

Both sexes have a light creamy-yellow triangle on the dorsal surface of segment 2. On the thorax the much reduced antehumeral stripes distinguish it from the Southern Hawker.

It is often seen flying in numbers along the sheltered margins of woodland, in contrast to Southern Hawkers which are usually seen alone.

Favoured habitat

The Migrant Hawker can be found at a range of aquatic habitat types wherever there are stands of emergent vegetation.

Bedfordshire: past and present

Despite the name the Migrant Hawker is common and widespread across Bedfordshire, breeding at lakes, ponds and rivers.

It was formerly known as the Scarce Aeshna and referred to by Cynthia Longfield as "*occuring locally but regularly in the southern counties of England, where it seems to have an isolated breeding post*"[1]. The name became somewhat of a misnomer as its numbers increased following a general trend of migrants from the continent. Even the change to 'Migrant' is questionable as it is now a widespread breeding species.

Palmer[2] records it as "*by no means common, though seems to be more abundant than A.juncea*". Records from 1942-1947 across the county would seem to suggest that it was already

widespread in the county during this period. First reported breeding in the sandpits at Leighton Buzzard[3]. It was recorded at Cardington Mill Pool and the staunch pool at Willington in the second week of October 1952[4]. Some years later it was reported as "*generally common on Ouse.*"[5] These early records suggest that over a period of 1942 to 1958 this species had become more widespread in the county. Early records from Hertfordshire suggest a similar situation where Palmer[6] described it as "*an uncommon species*".

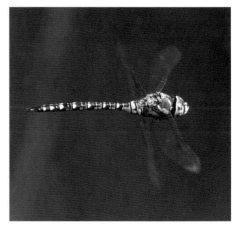

▶ Male Migrant Hawkers spend much of their time searching for females by flying in and out of stands of emergent vegetation by the water's edge. Priory CP, September 2003.

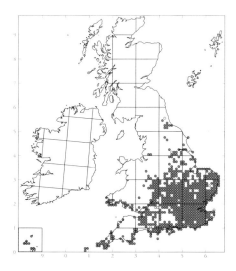

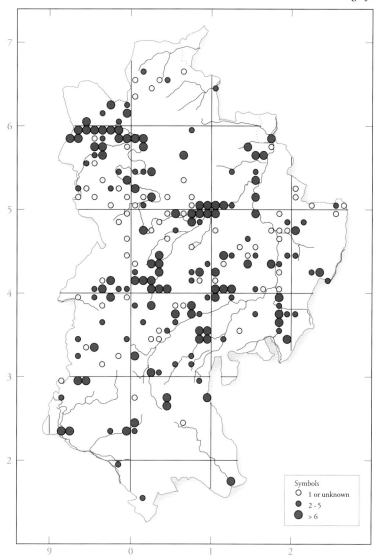

Symbols
○ 1 or unknown
◔ 2 - 5
● > 6

Conservation status

A proven breeding species at running and stillwater sites throughout the county. Where it occurs it appears in high numbers each year.

Field notes

Males are less territorial than other Hawkers with a number of males often present at the breeding sites. Males fly in and out of stands of emergent vegetation in search of females.

In late summer it can reach very high numbers. It generally flies higher than other hawkers.

It flies in shelter of trees and woodland often feeding in large numbers. Along sheltered hedgerows individuals can often be seen resting on bushes sometimes in close proximity to each other. They will fly close to bushes in search of prey and will pick off (gleaning) small insects from flowers or fruit. At Felmersham NR one male was seen taking small flies that were feeding on blackberries.

Females oviposit into plant stems and dried algae above water level. At Stewartby a female was observed ovipositing into dried algae some 10cm above dry mud and well away from water. At Sandhouse Pit in August 2003 another female was seen ovipositing into dried stems of Bulrush after the small ponds had dried up. A female was observed at Westminster Pond, Ampthill ovipositing into a Bulrush head three feet above the ground[7].

The larvae hatch from the eggs in early spring and have a rapid development enabling them to complete their life cycle in one year. This enables the species to colonise pools that dry out or where water levels drop appreciably during the late summer. Final instar larvae and exuviae are noticeably smaller than those of other hawkers.

Flight period

In Bedfordshire the flight period is typically from early July through to the second week of November.

First date   29th June
Last date   12th November

References

[1] Longfield (1937)

[2] Palmer (1947)

[3] Reid (1951)

[4] K.E.West (1952)

[5] K.E.West (1958)

[6] Palmer (1940)

[7] S. Plummer (pers. com.)

Emperor Dragonfly

Anax imperator

(Leach 1815)

Family: *Aeshnidae*

▲ Pair of Emperor dragonflies 'in-cop'.

Distinctive features

The Emperor Dragonfly is a large species that will often be the most aggressive species defending air space over water.

Males are very noticeable by the blue abdomen with a broad black dorsal stripe. The thorax of both sexes lacks the antehumeral stripes of other Hawker dragonflies.

Females tend to have a greeny-brown abdomen that can develop a blue tinge later in the season.

"he showed up grandly in the fierce sunlight, literally scintillating as he hung with vibrating wings over the water." [4]

Favoured habitat

Occurs at a range of well-vegetated lakes, large ponds, canals and slow moving rivers. Particularly favours habitat with plenty of submerged and floating vegetation where females can settle to oviposit.

Bedfordshire: past and present

Now widespread in Bedfordshire and probably still increasing its range.

Palmer [1] records it to be scarce in the county with no records of the species being captured. He also states that it is easily mistaken for a large *Aeshna* when seen at distance and probably overlooked. Later entries in his field notes give records for Flitwick Moor, June 1947, Heath and Reach, June 1947, Barton Hills, June 1948. In 1950 it was considered by D.A.Reid to be commoner than usual around Leighton Buzzard, *"far more abundant than usual"* [2]. It was also reported to be scarce in Hertfordshire at the time being recorded close to Bedfordshire at Knebworth and Oughton Head, Hitchin [3].

Conservation status

A proven breeding species in the county. Records indicate that it is extending its range northwards and becoming more abundant.

Field notes

Very territorial and very aggressive to other males. Males appear to be tireless flyers as they hawk back and forth along

References

[1] Palmer (1947)

[2] Palmer (1950a)

[3] Hine (1934)

[4] Lloyd, S. (1948)

[5] Parsons, D. (pers.com.)

► Female Emperor dragonfly ovipositing into Broad-leaved Pondweed.

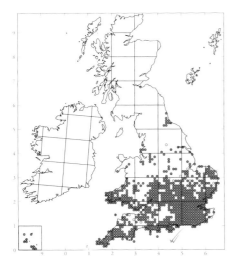

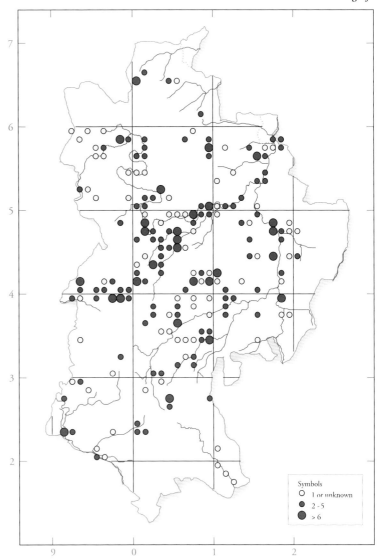

their territory. During 1990 at least five males were observed holding territory on the main pond at Flitton Moor. This is exceptional for a relatively small pond to hold this number of territorial males.

Females oviposit into floating vegetation, especially Broad-leaved Pondweed. They can often be observed prospecting for suitable oviposition sites. The low flight and arching abdomen is characteristic behaviour whilst the female attempts to avoid the attention of territorial males. Larval development usually takes two years in Bedfordshire although it has been known from elsewhere to devlop in one, when conditions are favourable.

During emergence larvae climb plant stems to emerge 30-50 cms above water surface. The larvae and hence the exuviae are very visible due to their large size. It typically emerges at night to avoid predation.

Females are usually much greener than males but occasionally develop the bright blue male colouration. During July 1991 a female of this colour form was photographed ovipositing at a pond at Haynes[5].

Flight period

In Bedfordshire from first week of June through to mid September.

First date   16th May
Last date   28th September

▼ Male Emperor Dragonfly in flight. Males of this species tirelessly patrol back and forth along a stretch of water in search of females. Note how the legs are tucked under the body to give it a more aerodynamic profile.

Broad-bodied Chaser

(Linnaeus 1758)

Libellula depressa

Family: *Libellulidae*

▲ A pristine female Broad-bodied Chaser. As they age, females tend to become a more drab brown colour.

Distinctive features

The Broad-bodied Chaser is a very distinctive dragonfly with its broad abdomen giving it a bulky appearance. Immature adults of both sexes are brown, with yellow abdomen and are often described as being Hornet (*Vespa crabro*) like.

When viewed from almost any angle the dark patches at the wing bases are very noticeable and a diagnostic feature of *Libellula* species. Rows of yellow spots along the sides of the abdomen are also very distinctive. As they mature the males develop blue pruinescence on the abdomen whereas the females go darker brown. Males have some superficial similarity to males of Scarce Chaser and Black-tailed Skimmer.

Favoured habitat

The Broad-bodied Chaser favours shallow stillwater habitat more than any other dragonfly in the county. This type of habitat is becoming increasingly rare to find in eastern England. Field ponds, where they still occur, are a favoured habitat.

Bedfordshire: past and present

The Broad-bodied Chaser has a scattered, widespread distribution across the county but nowhere would it be regarded as a common species. The shallow pools that form in quarries at Sundon Chalk Quarry SSSI, support strong breeding populations. Garden ponds are another favoured habitat especially in the absence of fish. Along the River Great Ouse it often breeds in shallow oxbow and overflow pools close to the river. It is most often recorded as single individuals as the distribution map clearly shows. The distribution and abundance of this species appear to have changed significantly since

Ray Palmer's time as recorder. He reported the Broad-bodied Chaser as "*The commonest and best known species and probably the most abundant large dragonfly in the county…Reported from farm ponds and ditches where other species are absent. Common at the peat bogs at Flitwick Moor*"[1]. "*generally common throughout the county, often breeding in remote farm ponds*"[2]. The same situation applied in Hertfordshire where it was

► Male Broad-bodied Chaser. Oakley, June 2003. This individual has not aquired the full blue colouration, which develops as a result of a waxy pruinescence on the surface of the abdomen.

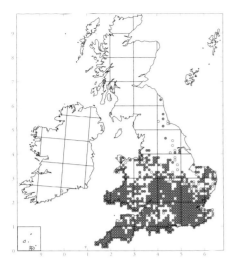

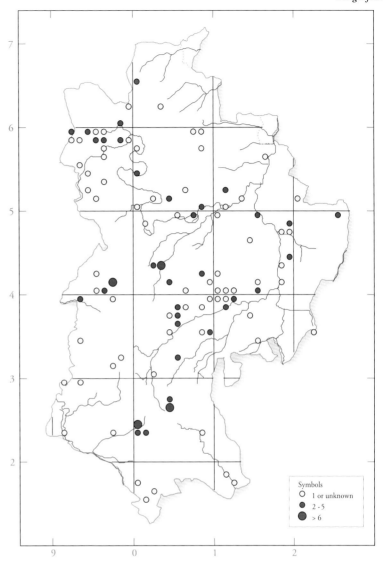

"*one of the commonest species, frequents ponds and ditches all over the county, sometimes occurring in large numbers in the spring*"[3].

Records began to decline to the point where Nancy Dawson in her time as recorder reported "*I could not find this species in Bedfordshire in the early 1970s*"[4]. She attributed this to the loss of farm ponds in the county but noted it possibly increasing again as a regular visitor to garden ponds.

Conservation status

The Broad-bodied Chaser is a proven breeding species in Bedfordshire. The loss of any shallow water habitat will have a negative impact on this species.

Field notes

The Broad-bodied Chaser is a great wanderer and will often turn up anywhere. Females oviposit alone by repeatedly dipping their ovipositor onto the water's surface and depositing eggs with each touch. The male sometimes hovers nearby guarding the female.

Larvae are very similar to those of the Four-spotted Chaser and found in mud and silt. They are very hairy which enables them to remain hidden when in search of prey. They usually take two years to develop. Emergence takes place during the day in vegetation close to the pond. Rushes and Spike-rushes are often the favoured support.

Following emergence adults can be seen perching in hedgerows in close proximity to each other during the maturation period. As the males reach maturity and return to the breeding site they become very territorial and aggressive to other males. They will immediately engage them in combat and 'chase' them out of their territory.

Flight period

In Bedfordshire it appears early in May and can be on the wing still in September in exceptional years.

| First date | 4th May |
| Last date | 23rd September |

References

[1] Palmer (1947)

[2] K.E.West (1958)

[3] Hine (1934)

[4] Dawson (1988b)

Four-spotted Chaser *Libellula quadrimaculata*

(Linnaeus 1758)   **Family:** *Libellulidae*

▲ The spots on the mid point of each wing make this an easily identifiable dragonfly.

Distinctive features

A medium sized dragonfly, so-named because of the distinctive dark spots mid-way along the leading edge of each wing.

A heavily marked form *praenubila* has dark patches at the end of the wings. Shortly after emergence it develops bright yellow wing veins but these darken with age. Later in the season it can appear quite drab.

There is a slight chance that Broad-bodied Chaser and Scarce Chaser females could be confused. Both of these species lack the dark spots on the wings.

Favoured habitat

The Four-spotted Chaser breeds at well vegetated pools across the county. It will breed in ponds, pools, lakes and occasionally on slower stretches of the county's rivers. The largest populations occur where there is a good diversity of submerged and emergent vegetation surrounded by shelter.

Bedfordshire: past and present

It is widespread across the county where it occurs mainly at stillwater sites but occasionally wanders over to the rivers. The pools at the north end of Coronation Pit currently support one of the largest breeding populations in the county. During early summer they are in great abundance and during May 2002 the author recorded hundreds of emerging adults around the margins of the small pools.

Records suggest that the species is now more abundant than ever. Palmer[1] reported it as a migratory species and a great wanderer. He quotes from a letter by C.Longfield "*Strangely I only have one recent record from the county, River Ouse - wings only* ". Recorded Flitwick Moor, 8th June 1947 and Biggleswade,

21st May 1948. Large numbers were recorded at Wavendon Heath on 30th May 1948[2]. In Hertfordshire Hine[3] recalls that he knew of no locality where it breeds except for a record of a single

▶ During the early stages of emergence there are no signs of the dark spots on the expanding wings. This individual was photographed during a 'mass' emergence at Felmersham NR on the 9th June 1996.

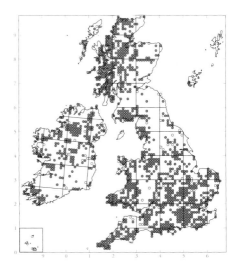

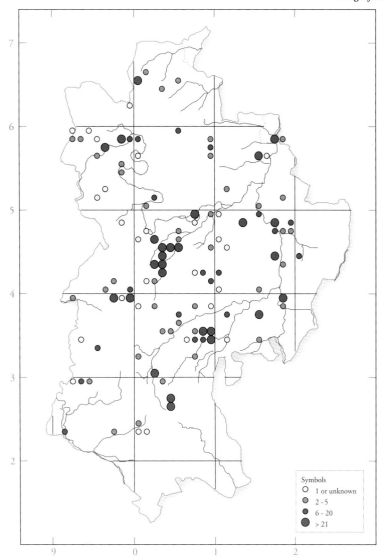

adult at Digswell near Welwyn.

Conservation status

A proven breeding species in the county. It tends to favour more mature habitat conditions and is likely to be adversely affected by clearance of emergent bankside vegetation and removal of fine detritus from the lake bed.

Field notes

The Four-spotted Chaser typically emerges in areas of Rushes and grass close to the water edge. Larvae climb these plants to the point where two stems cross enabling them to gain a good grip for the transformation process. There was a large synchronised emergence at Felmersham on 28th May 1992 and again on 9th June 1996, when numerous individuals were observed at several of the pools. Similar mass emergence has been observed at Coronation Pit over a number of years. Such behaviour often occurs on the first warm sunny day following a period of cooler overcast weather. The colours are usually very bright following emergence with the basal wing veins being bright yellow.

Females oviposit alone by dipping their abdomen on the water's surface whilst in flight. The eggs are sticky and float down through the water to become attached to underwater plants. Larvae are found in fine decomposing detritus on the bed of pond or lake and typically take two years to develop.

On 4th July 1993 one individual was observed at Harrold and Odell Country Park flying with only three wings, possibly the result of a bird attack. It appeared to be unaffected by the loss and was feeding and showing territorial behaviour.

Flight period

In Bedfordshire it has been on the wing at the end of April in an exceptionally warm spring through to the middle of September.

First date   30th April
Last date   17th September

References

[1] Palmer (1947)

[2] Palmer (1948)

[3] Hine (1934)

Scarce Chaser

(Müller 1764)

Libellula fulva

Family: *Libellulidae*

▲ Immature female Scarce Chaser showing bright orange colouration. Note the smoky wing tips that are characteristic of this species and are particularly prominent in females. River Great Ouse, May 1998.

Distinctive features

Following emergence both sexes are a bright orange colouration, which extends along the main wing veins. It is a very distinctive dragonfly during this maturation phase. Emergence is synchronised often resulting in a number of individuals being seen together in the meadows that surround the breeding site. As they become sexually active the orange colouration changes to powder blue in males and drab brown in females.

Mature males are most often encountered perched on prominent stems at the river bank. They have a pruinescent 'powder' blue abdomen similar to Black-tailed Skimmer. They can be distinguished from the latter by the presence of dark patches at the base of the wings.

Favoured habitat

The Scarce Chaser typically breeds in slow flowing rivers and dyke systems and occasionally in stillwater. Adult males can be seen holding territory along the riverbank and around lake margins. Lush meadow habitat surrounding the breeding site appears to be particularly important as a feeding area to this species.

Nationally it is a rare species and is associated with nine river systems in southern England[1]. In Bedfordshire it is restricted to one short length of the River Great Ouse as it leaves the county at Wyboston and a few of the nearby lakes. It has been proven to breed in the county both in the river and the lakes. It has been known for many years to breed along the River Great Ouse from St.Neots downstream to the Ouse Washes in Cambridgeshire. Some of the first confirmed breeding records for still water came from the gravel pit lakes at St.Ives, Cambridgeshire where

is was reported to have a preference for pits that are at least twenty years old[2]. These lakes are now very mature with luxuriant emergent and aquatic vegetation and extensive adjacent meadow land.

Bedfordshire: past and present

A relatively recent colonist to Bedfordshire. For many years it has been recorded from the River Great Ouse around Huntingdon and

▶ Scarce Chaser male showing characteristic abrasion marks on abdomen, resulting from the female grasping during mating

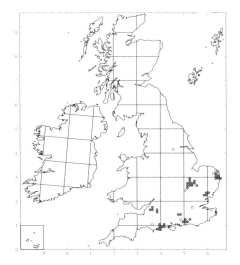

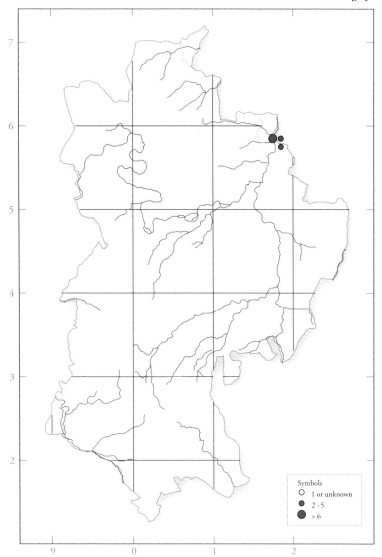

St.Ives and had been reported from Little Paxton and St.Neots close to the Bedfordshire border. Regular searches along the River Great Ouse at Wyboston and nearby sites failed to find it over a number of years. During early July 1998 it was finally recorded in Bedfordshire by the author, along the River Great Ouse and gravel pits next to the 'new' A428 flyover. This colony has now been observed regularly since its discovery and appears to be a self-sustaining breeding population. Males and females can be seen flying and settling over the rank vegetation between the river and lakes. Larvae have been found by 'pond dipping' along the river margins providing the first breeding records in the county. The river is used by pleasure craft along this stretch although this does not appear to affect the Scarce Chaser.

Symbols
○ 1 or unknown
● 2 - 5
⬤ > 6

In May 2003 emerging adults and exuviae were observed along one margin of one of the Wyboston lakes adjacent to the River Great Ouse. This was the first record of the species breeding in stillwater for the county.

The first record for the county was by Harcourt Bath[3] who reported a single specimen from Newnham in Bedford in one of the earliest publications on British dragonflies. No details are given in his book, but as he queries records for other species, that he had not seen himself, he appeared satisfied that the identification was correct. In addition, J.C.Dale's "calendar" has an entry for *Libellula conspurcata* on 31st May 1820. It states Newnham, Bedford and

◀ Two Scarce Chaser males perching together late in the season. Both show the typical abrasion marks caused by the female's legs during mating. Wyboston, June 1999.

▶ Female Scarce Chaser in 'feeding mode'. Note how the head has twisted so it can use its eyes to assess flying prey entering its air space. It will dart out to capture the prey, typically returning to the same spot to consume it. River Great Ouse, May 1999.

References

[1] Cham (2000)

[2] Milne (1984)

[3] Bath (1890)

[4] Longfield (1937)

[5] Palmer (1947)

[6] B.B. West (pers.com.)

[7] Cham (1999)

▼ Female Scarce Chaser at the end of the season, showing drab colouration and torn wing tips. Note the colour change from that shown in the above photograph Wyboston, July 1999.

that it was a specimen received from Mr. Bucklow. It would appear that these refer to the same specimen. Longfield[4] also quotes this record "*one record from Bedford*". Palmer[5] makes mention to the River Ouse at Huntingdon where it was found regularly between 1909 and 1913 although no records for Bedfordshire are mentioned.

The Scarce Chaser has a superficial similarity to the Black-tailed Skimmer with which it sometimes occurs. The occurrence of the latter at sites along the River Great Ouse has resulted in the need for careful examination of all individuals. This may explain unconfirmed reports[6] from Willington during the mid 1990s where the latter species is frequent.

Conservation status

Nationally it is a rare and potentially threatened species, confined to a small number of lowland river systems. This makes it very vulnerable to pollution incidents. It is listed as a Red Data Book species.

In recent years it has shown some signs of expanding its range. It is one of Bedfordshire's rarest species and of high conservation significance.

Field notes

Emergence takes place in dense vegetation within one metre of the water's edge. The adults are adept at crawling around in vegetation to ensure that they remain concealed. Both sexes go through age related colour changes during maturation.

During periods of poor weather or

overnight, Scarce Chasers roost low down in relatively dense vegetation. This not only shelters them from adverse weather conditions but avoids potential predation and disturbance while they are inactive[7].

"During late afternoon/evening, individuals of Libellula fulva *could be observed flying around sheltered parts of the meadow. They would make several attempts before finally resting. Early morning searches in these areas failed to find roosting individuals. If likely areas such as patches of Common Nettle were carefully studied for the first few hours after sunrise the rustling of dragonfly wings could be heard. This revealed the presence of* Libellula fulva *before any observation was possible. Within minutes individuals could be seen climbing up the nettle stems to catch the warmth of the rising sun. Once high up the stem they would rest for approximately 30 minutes before taking their first flight. These first flights were sluggish with frequent settling, usually allowing a very close approach (5cm away with a 20mm lens!). As the day progressed feeding flights became more active and individuals were less approachable. Similar observations have been made in patches of tall grass and umbellifers where* Libellula fulva *would suddenly 'appear' despite earlier searches revealing nothing."*

(Extract from author's field notes)

Copulation is much longer than other *Libellula* species, seldom lasting less than 15 minutes. During mating the legs of the female clasp the surface of the male's abdomen leaving dark marks where the pruinescence has been abraded. This is a useful sign that males have mated.

The larvae are very distinctive with a row of prominent dorsal spines along the abdomen. They can be found in mud around the roots of emergent vegetation along the river and lake margins. The best way to find them is to skim through the surface layers of mud using a net with a straight edge and

then spread the contents onto a plastic sheet. By watching carefully one can see the bulky larvae as they try to move out of the mud. Along the River Great Ouse the larvae are often found together with Black-tailed Skimmer larvae.

Flight period

A spring species with a synchronised emergence during May and sometimes into early June. In Bedfordshire it has been recorded from the middle of May through to the last week of June.

First date   18th May
Last date   28th June

▲ Searching for proof of breeding in Bedfordshire. The larvae of the Scarce Chaser live in the surface layers of mud surrounding emergent plant roots. A robust net is required to find them. River Great Ouse, Wyboston, April 2002.

▼ The first proof of breeding at stillwater habitat in Bedfordshire, Wyboston Lakes, 18th May 2003. A newly emerged adult can be seen at the lake margin close to the flyover. It was a dull day when this photograph was taken. Several emerging adults and exuviae were found well down in the vegetation.

Black-tailed Skimmer *Orthetrum cancellatum*

(Linnaeus 1758)   Family: *Libellulidae*

▲ Female Black-tailed Skimmer resting in a grass meadow at Felmersham NR, June 2000.

"Numerous individuals were emerging around the lake margins at Houghton Regis Chalk Pit. They were concentrated along the northern edge (south facing and thus the warmest side) with few being found elsewhere. Most were emerging on rushes at varying distances from the water. One exuvia was found 11 metres from the water's edge. This was an exceptional and highly synchronised emergence."

(Extract from authors field notes- 23rd May 1992)

▶ Powder blue male in 'typical' resting posture on light coloured surface. Sundon Chalk Quarry, July 2003.

Distinctive features

This is a medium sized dragonfly. Males have a characteristic habit of resting on bare ground, which can aid identification even from some distance. They appear powder blue resulting from pruinescence on the abdomen. Females and immature males are yellow with black markings. Females darken with age becoming drab brown.

It is possible to confuse powder blue males with males of Scarce Chaser, which has dark patches at the base of the wings. The Scarce Chaser perches on upright stems and will rarely if ever settle on the ground.

Favoured habitat

The Black-tailed Skimmer favours open stillwater sites with plenty of bare banks where males will settle. It is a rapid coloniser of newly created pools in mineral extraction quarries and will readily breed at new sites with minimal vegetation.

Bedfordshire: past and present

This species has undergone a dramatic range expansion over the last decade, which has been greatly facilitated by the creation of suitable habitat due to mineral extraction. It is now widespread across Bedfordshire especially on stillwater sites, as well as some lengths of the River Great Ouse.

In the past it has not always been as common as it is now. There were no early records for Hertfordshire[1]. Palmer[2] stated that it was found in Huntingdonshire, Cambridgeshire and Hertfordshire but not noted in Bedfordshire. Over subsequent years it was reported as "*not uncommon at Grovebury Pits, Leighton Buzzard, also common at Brickworks Pit, Stanbridge.*"[3]

The first recorded breeding record came from sandpits at Leighton Buzzard in 1951[4]. Dawson[5] reported that the species was on the edge of its range in Bedfordshire. This is certainly not the case now with records showing that its range has extended to Co. Durham and Northumberland[6].

Conservation status

The Black-tailed Skimmer is a proven breeding species in Bedfordshire and requires sites of an 'open' nature. If shading vegetation is allowed to get too dense it will disappear from a site.

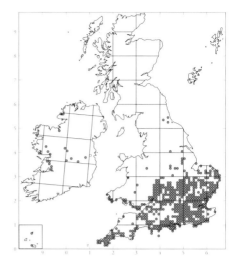

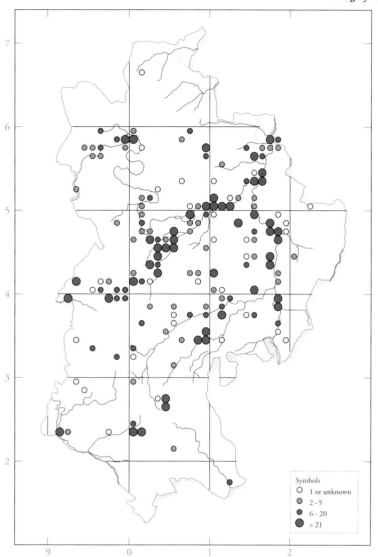

Field notes

Males can be observed flying low and fast (skimming) around pool margins settling at intervals on bare light coloured surfaces. It readily breeds at open quarry sites and has a synchronised emergence in early summer.

Tandem pairs will settle on the ground to complete copulation. Females oviposit by flying low over water and touching the end of the abdomen on the water's surface. The males guard the females during egg-laying. During July 2002 several females were photographed ovipositing at shallow pools at a gravel pit near Biggleswade. They would fly low to the water, dipping their abdomens into the water to deposit small clusters of eggs. In most cases the male would guard

Symbols
○ 1 or unknown
◔ 2 - 5
● 6 - 20
⬤ > 21

the female from the attention of other males. It appeared that the behaviour was necessary to avoid the repeated intervention of other conspecific males, as well as aggressive Four-spotted Chaser males. The attentions of the latter may be a result of mistaken identity as the females of the two species can look superficially similar.

Flight period

In Bedfordshire it is usually on the wing by late May flying to early September. In exceptional years it can go through to the end of September.

First date   15th May
Last date   25th September

References

[1] Hine (1934)

[2] Palmer (1947)

[3] Palmer (1950)

[4] Reid (1951)

[5] Dawson (1978)

[6] H.A Eales (pers.com.)

◀ A female in flight adopts a vertical posture of the abdomen, to avoid the unwanted attention of males. This is a form of female refusal behaviour that has not been documented before. Note the conspecific male attacking a male Four-spotted Chaser. Warren Villas, nr Biggleswade, July 2002.

Common Darter

(Charpentier 1840)

Sympetrum striolatum

Family: *Libellulidae*

▲ Pair of Common Darters 'in-cop'. Coronation Clay Pit, August 1999.

"It was a very hot afternoon when I called in at Stewartby village shop to buy an ice cream. As I stood by the car quenching my thirst, my attention was drawn to high numbers of dragonflies flying overhead. As I looked through binoculars I could see hundreds of Darter dragonflies flying at great height. Many of them were in tandem and appeared to be flying purposely in a north-easterly direction. They appeared to be dispersing from the north end of Rookery Pit. By dispersing in this manner the tandem pairs are ready to oviposit as soon as they arrive at a new site."

(Extract from author's field notes
1st September 1991)

▶ Male Common Darter 'sunning' itself on a garden clothes line.

Distinctive features

Females and immature males are yellow with black markings. Mature males develop through orange to a red colouration, whereas females become brown. The straight-sided abdomen and black legs with a yellow stripe distinguishes it from the closely related Ruddy Darter. Adult size is variable and one should not overlook the possibility of the superficially similar Vagrant Darter *Sympetrum vulgatum* appearing in Bedfordshire at some time.

The Common Darter is Bedfordshire's most abundant large dragonfly species.

Favoured habitat

The Common Darter lives up to its name as a very common and widespread species both in Bedfordshire and throughout Britain. There are very few freshwater habitats where this species does not occur at some time.

Bedfordshire: past and present

The Common Darter is a very abundant species in Bedfordshire being found all over the county. This appears to have always been the case. Palmer[1] regarded it as "*Very common and widespread, being found in all types of locality and very abundant at Flitwick Moor*". Longfield[2] also quoted it as "*common in Bedford*".

Hine[3] recalls that it was less numerous in Hertfordshire compared with other counties, and again noted it as very common in Bedfordshire, at Flitwick Moor "*Still very common and widespread*".

Conservation status

A very common breeding species with very little need for special management.

Field notes

This is a summer species with emergence spread out over the summer period. Because of the high numbers often present at a site many individuals can be observed emerging at the same time. On 16th July 2002 hundreds of exuviae were hanging on the rushes growing in the shallow pool margins close to the Forest Centre at the Marston Vale Country Park.

Following copulation pairs oviposit in tandem by flying low over the water. Eggs are scattered freely on the surface with each contact. There appears to be some form of deliberate site selection when ovipositing. Video recordings[4] at a pool in Rookery Pit showed that the male clearly 'steers' the female to selected areas. Eggs are laid over water

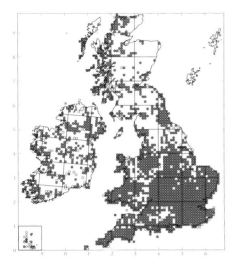

where vegetation is 'visible' below the surface. At first oviposition is directed by the male, but after a time the pair separate with the female continuing to oviposit alone or guarded by the male. At 'good' sites numerous tandem pairs can be seen ovipositing over water at the same time.

The larvae of Common Darter are active hunters. The shallow seepage habitat at Sundon Quarry is a good place to observe the larvae stalking invertebrate prey.

Common Darters are very efficient at dispersing and quick to colonise new sites. During the late summer of 1991 the author observed hundreds of Common Darters flying in tandem high over Stewartby village (see side notes).

In late summer as air temperature gets cooler large numbers can be seen resting on wire fences and clothes lines in gardens. They will often bask on bare ground in cool weather and

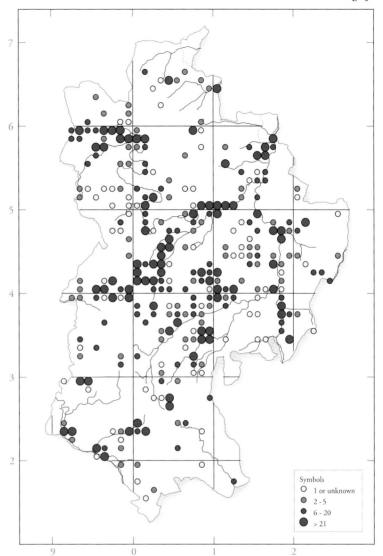

Symbols
○ 1 or unknown
◔ 2 - 5
● 6 - 20
● > 21

sometimes on clothing, camera bags and even cameras! (see p 7).

Flight period

In Bedfordshire the Common Darter has a very long season with an extended emergence period. It is on the wing in early summer and is usually the last species flying in late autumn. It typically starts to emerge in the middle of June and can still be found in the middle of November. The long flight period was also noted in former times by Palmer[5].

| First date | 15th May |
| Last date | 16th November |

References

[1] Palmer (1947)

[2] Hine (1934)

[3] Longfield (1937)

[4] Recorded on Hi8 video by the author and played back and analysed frame by frame.

[5] Palmer (1947)

◄ Tandem pair ovipositing over plant material lying in shallow water. They have a dual ovipositing strategy. Firstly, the male 'steers' the female in tandem, before breaking away to allow her to continue unaccompanied. Sundon, August 2003.

Ruddy Darter

(Müller 1764)

Sympetrum sanguineum

Family: *Libellulidae*

▲ Male Ruddy Darter ready to dart out from its perch to catch prey or see off rival males. Milton Bryan, August 2001.

Distinctive features

The Ruddy Darter is one of Bedfordshire's smallest dragonflies. It gets its name from the blood red colour of mature males. Females and immature males are yellow with black markings.

Males also have a distinctly 'waisted' club shaped abdomen (see page 112). This is less pronounced in females. Immature adults can be confused with other Darter species. The all black legs of both sexes distinguishes this species from the Common Darter, which is also slightly larger.

Favoured habitat

In Bedfordshire the Ruddy Darter is widespread at many stillwater sites, mainly ponds, ditches and small lakes with plenty of dense emergent vegetation. These conditions usually prevail at pools in the late stages of seral succession and prone to drying out in the summer. The short development time of the Ruddy Darter is well suited to such conditions. It is often found in association with the Emerald Damselfly, sometimes being the only two species present. It is increasingly being recorded along the slower stretches of the Rivers Great Ouse, Ouzel and Ivel where the banks are fringed with dense emergent vegetation.

Bedfordshire: past and present

In Bedfordshire it is now much more widespread than it used to be. Over the last two decades the Ruddy Darter has significantly expanded its range northwards and westwards in Britain; a trend that still appears to be continuing. In the first few years of the new millennium it was recorded in increasing numbers in Co. Durham and Northumberland, demonstrating

▶ Female Ruddy Darter ovipositing by 'throwing' her eggs onto vegetation surrounding a dried up pond. The eggs are flicked from the end of her abdomen as she flies in between the stems. Milton Bryan, August 2002.

its dramatic spread north. In some years numbers are supplemented by migration from the continent. Adults have been recorded along the east coast along with other migrant Darter species.

Palmer[1] regarded it as "*apparently rare but may be overlooked. Melchbourne Park lake August 1944, Turvey 1947*". A single male was recorded by Palmer at Battlesden Park Lake on 28th August 1948 and another at Bakers Wood, Heath and Reach on 28th August and 19th September. He also recorded it from Wavendon Heath ponds on 12th September 1951. These ponds are now dry and Palmer's notes also

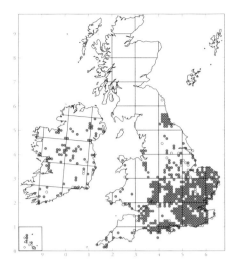

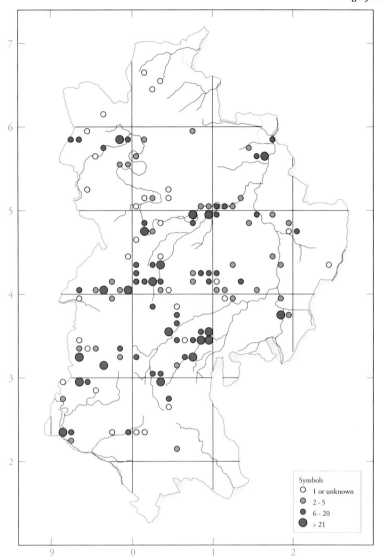

suggest a water shortage at the time. It was also recorded at Felmersham and Wyboston in 1948 and at Cople on 3rd June 1948[2]. Hine[3] had not recorded it for Hertfordshire further suggesting its rarity. It was referred to in 'Bedfordshire Wildlife'[4] as declining nationally, although this is in error as at the time it was expanding its range.

Conservation status

The Ruddy Darter is a proven breeding species in the county wherever suitable habitat exists. Any site management work needs to be undertaken with care. Removal of large stands of emergent vegetation, as is sometimes the case with pond cleaning activities, will destroy the favoured habitat conditions.

Field notes

The mating and egg-laying behaviour of this species is fascinating. After tandem formation mating takes place whilst perched and they remain 'in cop' for 20-30 minutes. The pair will rest before ovipositing commences. Tandem pairs are often observed ovipositing over damp mud and vegetation close to water. They can also be seen ovipositing over bare ground some distance from water. This at first appears to be a particularly risky strategy as there is a high probability of the eggs perishing. Females will often resume ovipositing alone after the

tandem has separated. A dual strategy enables the female to also select the oviposition site. Females will often egg-lay in areas of dense vegetation.

"At a series of seasonal ponds on the southern edge of Woburn Park I was attracted by the tell tale sounds of dragonfly wings brushing against vegetation. A number of Ruddy Darter females could be seen flying in and out of a dense area of Horsetail (Equisetum sp). The area was damp mud and very near to drying out completely. As they flew between the Horsetails they would hover and scatter eggs from a height of 30cms, with thrusting motions of the abdomen. Individual eggs could be clearly seen at the

▲ Ruddy Darters like to rest on light coloured surfaces. Sometimes they may not realise that a human might be attached! Sandhouse Quarry, August 2003.

▶ Ruddy Darters 'in cop'. Milton Bryan, August 2002.

References

[1] Palmer (1947)

[2] B.Verdcourt (pers.com.)

[3] Hine (1934)

[4] Nau *et al* (1987)

end of the female's abdomen being thrown onto the thin leaves and onto the ground. I was able to approach to within inches and able to take a series of photographs of them. This somewhat 'unusual' site selection behaviour is in anticipation of rising water levels during the winter."

(Extract from author's field notes August 2002)

To be able to survive at seasonal ponds that dry out in the summer this species has a very rapid larval development. The eggs laid in the previous summer's dry conditions are drought resistant and will overwinter in diapause. They hatch in early spring and larvae develop rapidly with adults emerging during June. It is thought that being adapted to such conditions also enables the larvae to avoid fish predation.

Males are very aggressive and will try to mate with any female that approaches the breeding area. Their high sex drive often leads to mistaken coupling, 'interspecific pairing', with females of Common Darter. This behaviour has been widely reported but can also lead to coupling with other males.

"A male Ruddy Darter was observed flying around in tandem with another

conspecific male. The primary male was trying to make the secondary male go through the motions of mating, as if it was a female. They would intermittently settle on the ground with one trying to mate and the other escape. Despite initial resistance this male became passive and allowed the primary male to fly in tandem and behave as if he had a female and was directing it to oviposit."

(Extract from author's field notes- Sandhouse Quarry August 2002)

As late summer air temperatures get cooler both sexes will often seek out warm reflective surfaces on which to bask. They can be observed sitting on bare reflective surfaces and will occasionally land on light coloured clothing and camera bags. By offering a carefully outstretched arm it is often possible to encourage them to settle on the back of one's hand.

Flight period

In Bedfordshire it starts to emerge in the middle of June and flies through to early October.

First date 13th June
Last date 17th October

Yellow-winged Darter   *Sympetrum flaveolum*

(Linnaeus 1758)   Family: *Libellulidae*

Distinctive features

Although very similar to the Common Darter, both males and females of this species are immediately distinguished by the broad yellow patch at the base of the wings.

Males are red in colouration and females develop from yellow to drab brown.

When seen in flight males appear very orange compared to the other species, due to the interplay of the coloured wing markings and the red abdomen.

Favoured habitat

This species typically favours damp meadows with lush grasses and rushes that flood during the winter. Little is known about favoured habitat in Britain.

Bedfordshire: past and present

There was a large immigration during early August 1995 when it was recorded over much of Britain. In Bedfordshire it was recorded at Willington for a period of several weeks. Whilst males predominated during this period, females were also seen, with several 'in cop' with males. Ovipositing was observed on several occasions in the damper areas of the meadow. In the same year there were 18 sightings in Hertfordshire also resulting in no sightings the following year. Follow-up visits to the meadow during 1996 failed to find any sign of emergence of adults. This was the same outcome as in all other sites in Britain where it had been seen ovipositing. As a migrant any attempts at breeding should be monitored in subsequent years.

Palmer[1] regarded it as "*A migratory species that may turn up anywhere, but no Bedfordshire records.*" He also recorded it in Hertfordshire[2] where a large immigration occurred in 1926. Hine[3] also recalls this immigration.

"*In August and September 1926 there was a large immigration and the species was recorded from many parts of the county. On September 12th in that year I found* Sympetrum flaveolum *in fair numbers around a piece of marshy ground in Bricket Wood and obtained several specimens. The great preponderance of males was particularly noticeable: out of dozens of these insects which I observed, only two were females, and these in very battered condition. This seems the only record of the species in the county.*"

Conservation status

A regular migrant to Britain from the continent. Despite the number of records there have been very few records of it overwintering in Britain. When breeding has been confirmed colonies have been very short lived. Microhabitat conditions influenced by climatic factors may limit the ability of this species to colonise in Britain.

▲ A male Yellow-winged Darter photographed at Willington Meadow during the mass UK immigration of August 1995.

References

[1] Palmer (1947)

[2] Palmer (1930)

[3] Hine (1934)

Black Darter

(Sulzer 1776)

Sympetrum danae

Family: *Libellulidae*

▶ Male Black Darter showing the very dark colouration characteristic of males of this species. Surrey, August 1995.

This small black dragonfly breeds at boggy pools. It is a highly dispersive species and can often occur at sites well away from suitable breeding habitat. It is a very rare visitor to the county. Currently it is unlikely that it would breed in Bedfordshire due to the lack of bog habitat.

B.B.West took two specimens at Bromham Park in 1943, one being confirmed by Cynthia Longfield[1]. These specimens were thought to be dispersing, as the habitat in the area was clearly unsuitable at the time[2].

There were a number of records at the Wavendon Heath ponds during September and October 1951 where it was reported as *"abundant, especially on the lower pond…Still on the wing with* A.cyanea *on 15th October 1951"*[3]. From the notes available it is difficult to determine whether this was a small migratory group that chanced upon the site or whether it persisted over subsequent years. The ponds in question did at one time support *Sphagnum* moss and were visually suitable. However, the encroachment of trees, especially Rhododendrons and the lack of sympathetic management have resulted in the site drying out.

Other Bedfordshire records include one captured at Willington Staunch pool by B.B.West[4]. More recently a single male was reported at Woodcrafts, Stevington in 1996[5].

There have also been a number of intermittent records for Hertfordshire over the last century with the most recent being at Hertford Heath during 2002[6]. None of these records have produced any evidence of breeding.

References

[1] Palmer (1947)

[2] B.B.West (pers.com.)

[3] Palmer (in lit)

[4] K.E.West (1958)

[5] B.Verdcourt (pers.com.)

[6] A.Reynolds (pers.com.)

Red-veined Darter

(Selys 1840)

Sympetrum fonscolombei

Family: *Libellulidae*

The Red-veined Darter is a migrant species that is recorded in most years somewhere in the British Isles. Several attempts at breeding in Britain have been successful, with both exuviae and emerging adults being recorded. However these colonies tend to be short lived and die out after one or two seasons. Palmer[1] predicted that it might be recorded in the county *"A migratory species that may turn up anywhere"*. It is possible that if current trends continue it could appear in Bedfordshire at any time.

An unconfirmed sighting of a solitary male Darter with red wings at Shuttleworth in 1991 may have been misidentification. It was reported in September, which is very late for the major influxes of this species. There can be some confusion with Common Darter, which exhibits darkening wing venation that appears red under certain lighting conditions.

During the 1990s there have been intermittent records for Hertfordshire.

Reference

[1] Palmer (1947)

Species with historical records

Golden-ringed Dragonfly *Cordulegaster boltonii*

(Donovan 1807)   Family: *Cordulegastridae*

The Golden-ringed Dragonfly favours small streams on the lowland heaths and bogs in southern counties and the upland bogs.

It has a mainly western and northern distribution. There are no known breeding colonies close to Bedfordshire. The lack of suitable habitat in the county and adjacent counties makes it unlikely for this species to be recorded other than as wandering individuals.

There have been sporadic records for this species from the county. Palmer[1] reports a single adult from West Wood, Knotting on 6th July 1947. Several members saw this at close quarters on a Bedfordshire Natural History Society field meeting. Palmer also notes that he knew of no records from surrounding counties. B.B.West records a single adult from Putnoe Wood in July 1948, which was captured and confirmed[2]. Dawson[3] reports a record of B.B.West of a 'migratory swarm' of this species at Felmersham gravel pits. B.B.West

also reported this, illustrated with a drawing in Ardea, the newsletter of the Wildlife Trust. These observations are particularly unusual as the normal egg-laying site is small streams with sandy, gravel beds, habitat which is not found at Felmersham. Furthermore, the species is not known to form migratory swarms.

"This would appear to be a migratory swarm amounting to many hundreds, as the insects hung from the trees and grass throughout the reserve…. egg-laying was observed……the hot summer is a possible reason for this unusual phenomenon."

(B.B.West's account from Felmersham)

It should be noted that the above record was not accepted by the national recording scheme for the national atlas.

During June 1993 an unconfirmed sighting in Sheerhatch Wood may have been this species[4].

In southern counties it starts to emerge late May and flies through to September.

▲ Male Golden-ringed Dragonfly. Hampshire, July 2002.

References

[1] Palmer (1947)

[2] Palmer (1948)

[3] Dawson (1975)

[4] M. O'Brien (pers.com.)

Vagrant Emperor   *Hemianax ephippiger*

(Burmeister 1839)   Family: *Aeshnidae*

A very rare migrant into Britain. Between mid February and early March 1988 there were a number of reported sightings of dragonflies on the wing at what is an exceptionally early time of year. These sightings coincided with a period of very mild weather, southerly winds and the arrival of Sahara dust. Most of the brief descriptions that accompanied these sightings were inconclusive when viewed in isolation. However a few were highly suggestive

and combined with the weather conditions at the time it would appear that there had been a large-scale arrival of this species from North Africa.

During February 1988 a large blue-brown dragonfly was reported from a garden below Blows Downs, Dunstable where it was observed chasing a bumblebee. Although the dragonfly was not caught, this sighting coincided with this influx and was almost certainly a Vagrant Emperor.

Downy Emerald

Cordulia aenea

(Linnaeus 1758)

Family: *Cordulidae*

▶ Male Downy Emerald, hovering while patrolling its territory around the lake margin at Moat Pond, Thursley, Surrey. June 1997.

The only Bedfordshire record for Downy Emerald was at Heath and Reach in early July 1951[1]. Mature well-established pools in woodland, such as those on country estates, are the favoured habitat of this species. It thought to have a 3-4 year life cycle, with the larvae associated with slowly decomposing leaf litter such as builds up in undisturbed lakes. Currently there is little suitable habitat in Bedfordshire. It occurs close to the county at sites in Oxfordshire, at Burnham Beeches, Bulstrode Park and Gerrards Cross in Buckinghamshire and at Epping Forest in Essex. It was formerly recorded at Hatfield Forest lakes. It also breeds at a single site in north-east Norfolk.

On 9th July 1995 Ian Dawson recorded a single male at one of the ponds at Yardley Chase, Northamptonshire, not far from the county boundary. The origin of this individual is unknown, as it is some distance from any known colony. It is generally a non-dispersive species which makes it unlikely to re-colonise sites from where it has disappeared.

Palmer[2] stated that whilst absent from Bedfordshire it had been recorded from Buckinghamshire, Hertfordshire and Northamptonshire. There are historical records at Knebworth Park, Hertfordshire on 11th June 1922 where "*a pair flying around the lake and occasionally settling high up on the fir trees*". It was also observed by Prof. A.E.Boyd at Radlett, Hertfordshire[3].

It typically has a mid-May to late July flight period in southern Britain.

If this species does reappear in the county it is most likely to turn up at mature lakes in woodland or parkland. Males typically fly around lake margins with regular hovering bouts at bays and inlets. The photograph shows a typical view of what might be expected.

References

[1] Reid (1951)

[2] Palmer (1947)

[3] Hine (1934)

Club-tailed Dragonfly

Gomphus vulgatissimus

(Linnaeus 1758)

Family: *Gomphidae*

This species is confined to a small number of river systems in Britain. It favours slow moving rivers with accumulation of mud and silt, which the larvae inhabit. The River Thames is the nearest, with records from Oxfordshire and Buckinghamshire. Following emergence adults can fly many kilometres from water and are often recorded in sunny woodland rides. There have been no recent records near to Bedfordshire and it remains an unlikely visitor.

There was a pre-1900 record for Bedfordshire. J.C.Dale's "*calendar*" records 1st June 1820 "*Clapham Park Wood*" This is an exceptional record many kilometres from any known colony or previous record. This location was a popular collecting and release site for lepidopterists at the time. Questions have been raised as to whether this record might have resulted from deliberate introduction.

Appendix 1

British Dragonfly Society Code of Practice on collecting dragonflies

2004—2009

Dragonflies have been in existence for at least 200 million years as members of the global ecosystem, but today human activities pose grave threats to their continued survival. The BDS is strongly committed to the conservation of these important and beautiful insects and acknowledges that dragonflies have the right to exist independently of human requirements. The Society promotes the study of dragonflies in ways that minimise interference with their behaviour and ecology.

- Environmental pollution and the destruction of habitats are by far the most important causes of damage to dragonfly populations. Collecting is very rarely a major issue, but BDS wishes to promote high standards of practice and responsible attitudes to such activities, hence the need for this Code.

- The main concern is to prevent significant damage to populations, especially those of rare and vulnerable species. Nonetheless, a balance has to be struck between conservation on the one hand, and encouraging study and the growth of knowledge on the other. For example, if children are not allowed to examine dragonflies at close quarters, they may be less likely to engage with them, and thus may not develop concerns about their conservation; equally, some recording activities, educational and scientific research needs may legitimately require the taking of specimens.

This Code is commended as best practice by the Board of the British Dragonfly Society. An Appendix to this Code, available on the website, gives guidance on the legal and conservation status of dragonflies in Britain and Ireland.

* '**Collecting**' in this document means 'the taking of specimens for close examination': it embraces a wide range of situations — from the temporary capture and release of live insects (e.g. for identification) to the formation of study collections, which may necessitate killing and preserving specimens.

Principle 1: Live dragonflies should only be held captive for good reasons

Relevant circumstances

- Identification is not always straightforward, and it is often necessary to make close examination of specimens in the hand. Many identifications can also be achieved by observation, photography and collecting exuviae (larval skins). All UK species, but not all migrants, can be identified as adults or larvae without killing, using good identification guides.

- Live material of any stage might reasonably be required for such purposes as: breeding and other scientific studies; demonstration purposes- e.g. at field meetings or for brief educational display; photography/filming for publication, film or exhibition work; introductions and translocations for conservation purposes.

Guidelines:

1.1 For close inspection, it is possible, with care, to capture adult and larval dragonflies, examine them and release them undamaged. They should be released as soon as possible afterwards. When netting adult dragonflies, use techniques that minimise risks of killing them: sweeping upwards from behind or below is safest. Live material should be collected by or under the supervision of competent individuals who have appropriate fieldwork experience. The insect welfare implications of capture and handling should be explained, especially to children.

1.2 Release back into the wild should always be into sites at which the species occurs, except in the case of authorised translocations (see Guideline 1.3 below). Following longer-term projects, such as captive rearing, specimens should be returned to the wild whenever possible, at appropriate sites, in appropriate numbers and at suitable seasons. Rearing of larvae under conditions that could result in premature emergence should be avoided where possible.

1.3 Translocations and re-introductions should only be carried out after a thorough assessment of the feasibility of proposals. Advice of appropriate conservation bodies, including the BDS Dragonfly Conservation Group, must always be sought.

Principle 2: Dragonflies should only be killed when a justifiable and useful purpose is served thereby.

Relevant circumstances

* When voucher specimens of adults or larvae are needed to ensure the accurate identification of a difficult or unexpected species, and especially when alternatives such as field notes and/or photographs alone would not suffice. (Vouchers provide permanent physical evidence enabling identifications to be reconsidered by experts at different times, and in the light of developing knowledge.)

* When specimens are necessary for well-planned and justifiable scientific research and survey projects.

* Museum collections: national and major regional public museums with entomological staff need to hold study collections of Odonata. These serve to ensure that material from different time periods and geographical areas is available in the long term for research in the light of developing technologies and knowledge; voucher specimens of species new to the respective countries or regions may often be required.

Guidelines:

2.1 Voucher specimens: in any one instance a single specimen, male if possible, will often suffice. Such specimens should be permanently deposited in public collections whenever possible.

2.2 Where tissue sampling (e.g. for molecular analysis) is a practicable alternative to killing, this should always be considered.

2.3 Scientific research and survey projects: the ultimate deposition of research specimens and associated documentation in an appropriate public institution may be expected to be a part of such plans. The BDS Dragonfly Conservation Group should also be informed.

General points to be observed in fieldwork

The following is adapted from the *Code for Insect Collecting* originally formulated by the Joint Committee for the Conservation of British Insects in 1972:

* Observe relevant rules and regulations: collecting must not be carried out in contravention of any national Law, International Convention or Directive on conservation of species or habitats applying to the area; bye-laws and rules affecting collecting on nature reserves and protected areas must be observed.

* Always seek permission from the landowner or occupier when working on private land. Conditions laid down by the grantors of permission must always be respected.

* Do not take more specimens than are strictly necessary for any purpose.

* Supply details of the species noted, and any other relevant data, to those responsible for managing sites when collecting on sites of conservation interest.

* Be sensitive to the incidental damage that fieldwork may cause. When collecting exuviae during emergence periods, be sensitive to the disturbance to dragonflies at this critical stage. Submerged vegetation that has been worked for larvae should not be left on the bank, but should be replaced in the water. The needs of other organisms (e.g. fragile marginal vegetation, nesting birds and rare species generally) must be carefully considered, as must the interests of other users and occupiers of the countryside.

* Exercise discretion when passing on, or making public, the location of rare and vulnerable species.

* Do not collect specimens (other than exuviae) for exchange or disposal to other collectors, or for commercial purposes (e.g. for use in manufacture of decorative artefacts).

Collecting in public situations generally

🪰 Whenever collecting is done in front of an audience, for example, the Press and Media, a BDS Field Meeting, or simply those assembled to watch, there is potential for adverse reaction. The causes of such reactions will vary from simple misunderstandings to deeply held beliefs and other highly personal agendas. There will increasingly be issues where legitimate collecting may conflict with the needs of an 'audience' that has assembled to enjoy the spectacle of a rare or vagrant species — especially where the onlookers may have invested much time and effort to achieve their objectives.

🪰 Collecting alone under such circumstances should be avoided where possible, as should aggressive behaviour however much provoked. Whilst not to be expected, the possibility of physical abuse from the onlookers should not be entirely discounted.

Adverse public relations could quickly damage BDS and are to be avoided wherever possible. Collectors should beware that all activities may be recorded by the onlookers and the images and sounds rapidly transmitted elsewhere.

'Vagrant' here means any species, usually in low numbers, occurring at a location distant from its known breeding range.

Guidelines:

1　Before collecting, anyone acting for BDS, or who could reasonably be construed to be doing so, should obtain all necessary prior permissions, and either:

2　Give a clear explanation of the scientific purpose of the intended collecting, and try to ensure that this is understood and accepted by the onlookers, or...

3　If 2 above does not succeed, exercise judgement on whether to collect or not. If collecting does not proceed, give a reasoned and calm explanation of the potential loss to science that would ensue. A written record of the incident should be made, the names and behaviour of 'objectors' noted if possible, and a report submitted promptly to the Dragonfly Conservation Group.

The best interests of the BDS as a national body promoting conservation should be the overriding consideration when collecting in public situations.

Advice on the interpretation of this code:

Please contact the BDS Conservation Officer and/or the convener of the Society's Dragonfly Conservation Group. Contact details are on the BDS web-site: http://www.dragonflysoc.org.uk.

Review:

This code will be reviewed at least once every five years: next review: by November 2008

British Dragonfly Society, 2003.

Appendix 2

Plant names used in the text

Amphibious Bistort	*Persicaria amphibia*
Branched Bur-reed	*Sparganium erectum*
Broad-leaved Pondweed	*Potamogeton natans*
Bulrush	*Typha latifolia*
Bulrush species	*Typha spp.*
Bur-reed species	*Sparganium spp.*
Canadian Waterweed	*Elodea canadensis*
Common Club-rush	*Schoenoplectus lacustris*
Common Nettle	*Urtica dioica*
Common Reed	*Phragmites australis*
Common Spike-rush	*Eleocharis palustris*
Common Water-crowfoot	*Ranunculus aquatilis*
Duckweed species	*Lemna spp*
Fringed Water-lily	*Nymphoides peltata*
Hard Rush	*Juncus inflexus*
Jointed Rush	*Juncus articulatus*
Lesser Spearwort	*Ranunculus flammula ssp. flammula*
Mare's-tail	*Hippurus vulgaris*
New Zealand Pigmyweed	*Crassula helmsii*
Pondweeds	*Potamogeton spp.*
Reed Canary-grass	*Phalaris arundinacea*
Reed Sweet-grass	*Glyceria maxima*
Rigid Hornwort	*Ceratophyllum demersum*
Rush species	*Juncus spp.*
Sedge species	*Carex spp.*
Sphagnum mosses	*Sphagnum spp.*
Soft-rush	*Juncus effusus*
Water Fern	*Azolla filiculoides*
Water-lilies	*Nyphaea alba, Nuphar lutea & Nymphoides peltata*
Water-milfoils	*Myriophyllum spp.*
Water Mint	*Mentha aquatica*
White Water-lily	*Nyphaea alba*
Yellow Iris	*Iris pseudacorus*
Yellow Water-lily	*Nuphar lutea*

Marking dragonflies for Capture-mark-recapture (see page 13).

Acrylic paint (Humbrol Colour) can be used to mark the wings of larger dragonflies. It is water-based and quick drying and water resistant when dry. By using different colours and a combination of dots on each wing it is possible to uniquely mark individuals so they can be identified at a later stage. By carefully using a long handled camel hair brush with a fine tip it is possible to touch a small dot on the wings, without disturbing them.

For smaller damselflies, a number or dot pattern can be applied to the wings using free flowing indelible ink pens (Lumocolor). Following capture with a soft net the individual can be gently held with the finger tips while the marking is applied to the wings.

NB On no account should this be done on newly emerged adults as it will damage their fragile wings.

Appendix 3

Bedfordshire Dragonfly sites with more than 15 species

#	Site name	Grid reference (site centroid)	Banded Demoiselle	Emerald Damselfly	White-legged Damselfly	Large Red Damselfly	Blue-tailed Damselfly	Scarce Blue-tailed Damselfly	Common Blue Damselfly	Azure Damselfly	Red-eyed Damselfly	Small Red-eyed Damselfly	Hairy Dragonfly	Brown Hawker	Southern Hawker	Migrant Hawker	Emperor Dragonfly	Broad-bodied Chaser	Scarce Chaser	Four-spotted Chaser	Black-tailed Skimmer	Common Darter	Ruddy Darter	Species total
1	Bromham Lake NR/River Great Ouse**	TL027514	D	A	D	A	D		F	D	A	B	B	D	B	C	B	C		C		D	B	16
2	Coronation Clay Pit, Kempston Hardwick***	TL032436	B	D	B	F	F		F	F	E		B	D	C	E	C	F		F	F	F	D	18
3	Cow Pond, Haynes*	TL083422	A	D		C	D		E	E	E		B	A	A	C	B	C		C	B	D	C	16
4	Duck End NR, Maulden*	TL052374	B	C		D	C		D	D	C		A	B	B	C	B	C		C	A	C	C	16
5	Felmersham NR/River Great Ouse***	SP990583	C	C	D	D	F		F	E	F	B	C	D	C	E	B	C		E	D	E	C	19
6	Flitton Moor/River Flit*	TL056360	B	B		E	E		E	E	C	C	C	B	B	B	C	B		B	A	E	E	17
7	Harrold and Odell CP/River Great Ouse**	SP960568	C			C	E		E	E	E		D	A	C	C	B	A		C	C	E	C	15
8	Priory CP/River Great Ouse***	TL077492	F	B	C	C	F		E	F	E	E	B	D	B	D	C	B		D	D	E	E	19
9	Randalls Farm Environmental Centre*	TL020438	D		B	B	D		D	E	C		B	B	B	C	C	A		B	C	C	B	15
10	River Great Ouse, Bromham Hall*	TL012508	E	A	E	C	E		D	C	D		D	B	B	B	B	B		B	B	D	A	16
11	South Mills Gravel Pit, Sandy/River Ivel**	TL155501	C	B	B	C	E		F	B	D		C	C	C	D	B	B		C	D	D	C	17
12	Sundon Chalk Quarry***	TL042272	B	E	E	C	E	C	E	D	D	C	D	D	B	D	C	C		D	E	D	C	19
13	Tiddenfoot Sand Pit complex, Leighton Buzzard**	SP913235	B	B		B	D		F	D	B	C	D	D	B	C	B	A		B	D	D	B	16
14	Wrest Park, Silsoe***	TL092350	B		C	D	F		F	F	F	D	D	D	B	E	C	A		E	E	E	E	16
15	Wyboston Lakes Complex/River Great Ouse***	TL177579	E	E	E	B	E		F	D	F	C	C	C	D	D	C	D	C	D	E	D	B	16

Table shows highest estimate of numbers for each species based on RA70 recording card estimate of numbers:

A	1 only
B	2-5
C	6-20
D	21-100
E	100-500
F	>500

*** Sites of regional dragonfly importance
** Sites of county dragonfly importance
* Sites of local dragonfly importance

Appendix 4

Relative abundance of Bedfordshire Dragonfly species

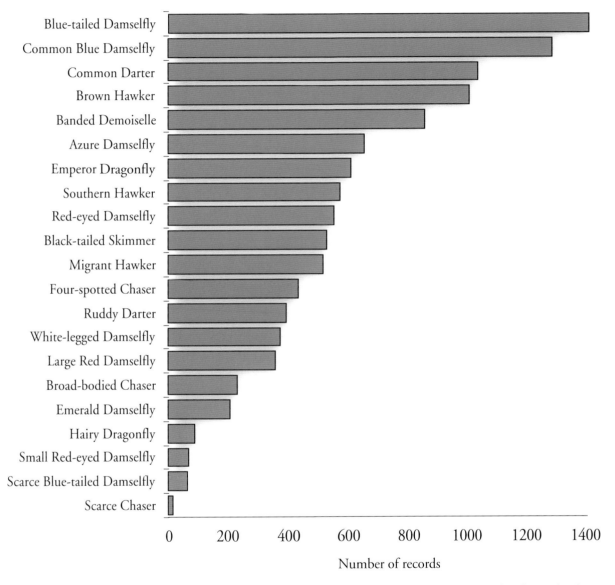

Number of records

▲ Chart showing the relative abundance of Dragonfly species in Bedfordshire, based on all records of adults between 1985 and 2003.

Appendix 5

Breeding maps for common Bedfordshire Dragonfly species

Whilst it would be desirable to plot maps showing the breeding status of the county's Dragonflies, the low number of records providing proof of breeding would result in a misleading picture. The maps for the four common species shown here illustrate this and should be compared with the maps in the individual species accounts.

▶ Banded Demoiselle
▶▶ Southern Hawker

▶ Common Blue Damselfly
▶▶ Common Darter

Breakdown of records on the Bedfordshire Dragonfly database by RA70 criteria:

Ad	72%
Co	9%
Ov	11%
La	1%
Ex	3%
Em	4%

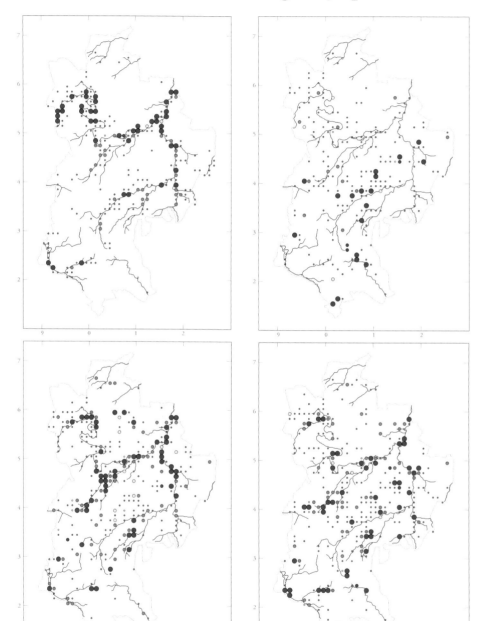

Key
● Pre-flight emergent or exuvia
● Larva
● Ovipositing female
○ Copulating pair
· Adult
○ unknown

The maps show breeding status as defined by the criteria on the RA70 card (see p11). The largest dots are for records where either exuviae or emerging adults have been recorded and thus the species has successfully bred. The smallest dots represent adult only records. The low percentage of larval records (1%) is indicative of the low recorder time spent on this activity.

Appendix 6

Useful addresses and websites

Bedfordshire Natural History Society - for membership details
c/o Bedford Museum, Castle Lane, Bedford, MK40 3XD
http://www.bnhs.org.uk/

British Dragonfly Society - for membership details
c/o The Haywain, Hollywater Road, Bordon, Hants GU35 0AD
http://www.dragonflysoc.org.uk/

The Dragonfly Project (formerly the National Dragonfly Biomuseum) - a mine of
information for all things relating to dragonflies
www.dragonflyproject.org.uk

Dragonflies and Damselflies in the UK - particularly in North Buckinghamshire
- for information on species in neighbouring counties
http://www.ghmahoney.org.uk/dragonfly/index.htm

English Heritage (Wrest Park) - for visiting arrangements to Wrest Park, Silsoe
http://www.english-heritage.org.uk

English Nature - for information on National Nature Reserves (NNRs) and Sites
of Special Scientific Interest (SSSIs)
Bedfordshire and Cambridgeshire Team
Ham Lane House, Ham Lane, Nene Park, Orton Waterville, Peterborough
PE2 5UR
beds.cambs@english-nature.org.uk
http://www.english-nature.org.uk

Environment Agency - good for information about the county's rivers and streams
http://216.31.193.171/asp/1_introduction.asp

Hertfordshire Dragonflies - for information on species in neighbouring counties
http://geocities.com/hertsdragonflies/

National Biodiversity Network - search for data on species, with interactive maps
http://www.nbn.org.uk/
http://www.searchnbn.net/

**The Wildlife Trust for Bedfordshire, Cambridgeshire, Northamptonshire and
Peterborough** - good for information on local nature reserves
Bedford Office, Priory Country Park, Barkers Lane, Bedford, MK41 9SH
http://www.wildlifetrust.org.uk/bcnp/

Worldwide Dragonfly Association - for further information on dragonflies both
UK and global
http://powell.colgate.edu/wda/dragonfly.htm

Glossary

Anal appendages	projections of varying sizes from the terminal segment of the abdomen. In males they are used to hold the female in tandem during mating and in some species during egg laying
Antehumeral stripes	stripes on the dorsal surface of thorax. Usually pale in colour
Caudal lamellae	fan-like structures at the end of the abdomen of damselfly larvae
Conspecific	of or relating to the same species
Costa	the thickened vein at the leading edge of each wing
Diapause	a period of suspended growth or development. Usually occurs in the egg and larval stages. Typically occurs over the winter period. Diapause in the egg enables species to survive unfavourable conditions. Development continues with the onset of more favourable conditions in the spring
Endophytic	describes mode of ovipositing into plant tissue (see also exophytic)
Eurytopic	occupying a wide range of habitat types (cf. stenotopic)
Eutrophic	aquatic habitat enriched with nutrients
Exophytic	describes mode of ovipositing on the suface of the water or substrate (see also endophytic)
Hawking	flying backwards and forwards
Instar	stages in larval development. The duration of the first instar is usually short and associated with the hatching of the egg. The final instar is the stage from which the adults emerge
Mask	the labium or lower lip of the larvae used to capture prey
Nymph	old term used for larva. No longer in widespread use
Oviposition	the process of laying eggs through the ovipositor
Ovipositor	organ at tip of female abdomen used for egg laying

Pruinescence	a waxy bloom that develops on the body of some species as they mature
Pseudo-pterostigma	a false pterostigma (found in British *Calopteryx* species)
Pterostigma	a small thickened patch towards the end of the leading edge of each wing. Often forms a darker 'spot'. Thought to play a role in counterbalancing the wing
Secondary genitalia	organ on the ventral surface of second abdominal segment of males
Semivoltine	completing one generation every two years
Sperm competition	the process whereby the last sperm received by the female is most likely to fertilise the eggs. Structures in the males secondary genitalia enter the female and displace sperm from an earlier mating before insemination
Sperm removal	also known as sperm displacement (see sperm competition)
Spring species	species usually with an early synchronised emergence period (see also Summer species)
SSSI	Site of Special Scientific Interest
Stenotopic	restricted to a narrow range of habitat conditions (cf. eurytopic)
Summer species	species with an extended emergence period. They emerge later and with less synchronisation than spring species
Tandem	used to describe a male coupled with a female either prior to or immediately following copulation. In some species the tandem coupling lasts during egg laying
Teneral	used to describe a newly emerged adult while the wings are still hardening. Not to be confused with immature
Univoltine	completing one generation in one year
Vulvar scale	a small flap on 8th abdominal segment of females in some species. Can be useful for identification

Bibliography and References

Abbot, C. (MS) *Lepidoptera Anglica cum Libellulis.* Hope Library, Oxford. (Dale 23).

Abbot, C. (1798) *Flora Bedfordiensis.* Smith, Bedford.

Adams, J.M. (1945) *Bull.Amat.Ent.Soc.* 6:42

Anderson, D. & Anderson, K. (2002) Dragonflies 2001 *Bedfordshire Naturalist* **56**, 68-70.

Arnold, V.W., Baker, C.R.B., Manning, D.V. and Woiwood, I.P. (1997) *The Butterflies and Moths of Bedfordshire.* The Bedfordshire Natural History Society.

Bath, W. Harcourt (1890) *Illustrated Handbook of British Dragonflies.* The Naturalists Publishing Co.

Benton, E. (1988) The dragonflies of Essex. *Essex Naturalist* **9**, Essex Field Club.

Brooks, S. (1997) *Field Guide to the Dragonflies and Damselflies of Great Britain and Ireland.* British Wildlife Publishing, Hants.

Brooks, S. (2002) *Field Guide to the Dragonflies and Damselflies of Great Britain and Ireland.* Revised edition, British Wildlife Publishing, Hants.

Cham, S.A. (1990) *Bedfordshire Dragonflies. A provisional atlas of the dragonflies of Bedfordshire* . Bedford Museum, North Bedfordshire Borough Council.

Cham, S.A. (1990) A study of *Ischnura pumilio* (Charpentier) with particular reference to the state of maturity of the female form *aurantiaca.* *J.Br.Dragonfly Soc.* Vol. **6**, 42-44

Cham, S.A. (1991) The Scarce Blue tailed Damselfly *Ischnura pumilio* (Charpentier) its habitat preferences in south-east England. *J.Br.Dragonfly Soc.* **7**, 18-25

Cham, S.A. (1992) Ovipositing behaviour and observations on the eggs and prolarvae of *Ischnura pumilio* (Charpentier) *J.Br.Dragonfly Soc.* **8** (2), 6-10

Cham, S.A. (1993) Further observations on generation time and maturation of *Ischnura pumilio* with notes on a mark-recapture programme. *J.Br.Dragonfly Soc.* **9** (2), 40-46.

Cham, S.A. (1996) The Scarce Blue-tailed Damselfly- the conservation of a wandering opportunist. *British Wildlife* 7 (4), 220-225

Cham, S.A. (1999) Roosting behaviour of some British Odonata with notes on the Scarce Chaser *Libellula fulva* Muller. *J.Br.Dragonfly Soc.* **15** (2), 58-60.

Cham, S.A. (2000) Discovery of a 'new' population of the Scarce Chaser *Libellula fulva* (Muller) on the River Stour in the Dedham Vale. *J.Br.Dragonfly Soc.* **16** (1), 17-19.

Cham, S.A. (2001) The status of the Small Red-eyed damselfly *Erythromma viridulum* (Charpentier) in the British Isles *Atropos* **12**, 7-9

Cham, S.A. (2002) The range expansion of the Small Red-eyed damselfly *Erythromma viridulum* (Charp.) *Atropos* 15:3-9

Cham, S.A. (2002b) *Dragonfly survey of selected Wildlife Trust reserves in Bedfordshire.* Report for the Wildlife Trust for Bedfordshire, Cambridgeshire, Northamptonshire and Peterborough.

Cham, S.A. (2002c) Mate guarding behaviour during intense competition for females in the Common Blue Damselfly *Enallagma cyathigerum* (Charpentier). *J.Br.Dragonfly Soc.* 18 (1 & 2) 46-48.

Cham, S.A. (2003a) The Small Red-eyed damselfly *Erythromma viridulum* in Bedfordshire 2002. *Bedfordshire Naturalist* 57 (Part 1):

Cham, S.A. (2003b) Factors influencing the distribution of the White-legged Damselfly *Platycnemis pennipes* (Pallas) in Great Britain. *J.Br.Dragonfly Soc.* **19** (1 & 2) 15-23.

Cham, S.A. & Banks, C. (1986) Unusual feeding behaviour by *Aeshna grandis* (L.) *J.Br.Dragonfly Soc.*, **2** (1), 43-44.

Cham, S., Brooks, S.J. & McGeeney, A. (1995) Distribution and habitat of the Downy Emerald Dragonfly *Cordulia aenea* (L.) (Odonata: Corduliidae) In Britain and Ireland. *J.Br.Dragonfly Soc.*, 11 (2), 31-35.

Comont, J. (1988) *Ischnura pumilio* (Scarce Blue-tailed Damselfly) in Bedfordshire. *Bedfordshire Naturalist* **42**, 59.

Corbet, P.S. (1999) *Dragonflies - Behaviour and ecology of Odonata.* Harley Books, Colchester.

Corbet, P.S., Longfield, C. & Moore, N.W. (1960) *Dragonflies.* New Naturalist. Collins. London.

Dawson, N. (1974) Dragonflies of Bedfordshire- A survey of old records. *Bedfordshire Naturalist* **29**, 50-53.

Dawson, N. (1976) Dragonflies (Odonata) Report of the Recorder (for 1974). *Bedfordshire Naturalist* **29**

Dawson, N. (1976) Dragonflies of Bedfordshire - A guide to their identification. Bedfordshire Natural History Society

Dawson, N. (1977) Dragonflies (Odonata) Report of the Recorder (for 1975). *Bedfordshire Naturalist* **30**, 22-23.

Dawson, N. (1977) Dragonflies (Odonata) Report of the Recorder (for 1976). *Bedfordshire Naturalist* **31**, 47-49.

Dawson, N. (1979) Dragonflies (Odonata) Report of the Recorder (for 1978). *Bedfordshire Naturalist* **33**, 51.

Dawson, N. (1980) Dragonflies (Odonata) Report of the Recorder (for 1979). *Bedfordshire Naturalist* **34**, 37.

Dawson, N. (1981) Dragonflies (Odonata) Report of the Recorder (for 1980). *Bedfordshire Naturalist* **34**, 37.

Dawson, N. (1982) Dragonflies (Odonata) Report of the Recorder (for 1981). *Bedfordshire Naturalist* **36**, 41.

Dawson, (1987) Dragonflies (Odonata) Report of the Recorder (for 1986). *Bedfordshire Naturalist* **41**, 65.

Dawson, N. (1988a) Dragonflies (Odonata) Report of the Recorder (for 1987). *Bedfordshire Naturalist* **42**, 57-59.

Dawson, N. (1988b) Forty years on: a comparison of the dragonfly fauna of Bedfordshire in the 1940s with the situation today. *J.Br.Dragonfly Soc.* **4** (2), 25-28.

Dewick, S. & Gerussi, R. (2000) Small Red-eyed Damselfly *Erythromma viridulum* (Charpentier) found breeding in Essex - the first British records. *Atropos* **9**, 3-4

Dijkstra, K.D.B., Kalkman, V.J., Ketelaar, R. & Van Der Weide, M.J.T. (2002) *De Nederlandse Libellen (Odonata)* National Natuurhistorisch Museum Naturalis KNNV Uitgeverij

Dony, J.G. (1953) *Flora of Bedfordshire.* Corporation of Luton Museum and Art Gallery

Dony, J.G. (1967) *Flora of Hertfordshire* Hitchin Museum and Art Gallery, Hitchin

Dony, J.G. (1972) A new system of recording for Bedfordshire. *Bedfordshire Naturalist* **2**, 58-61

Dony, J.G. (1976) *Bedfordshire Plant Atlas.* Borough of Luton Museum and Art Gallery.

Doubleday, H.A. & Page, W. (Eds) (1904) *The Victoria History of the county of Bedford.* Constable, Westminster.

Driver, A. 1997 River and Wetland Rehabitation in the Thames Catchment. *British Wildlife* **8** (6), 362-372.

Evans, M.W.F. (1845) *British Libellulinae or dragonflies.* Bridgewater, London

Fox, A.D. (1989) *Ischnura pumilio* (Charpentier) (Odonata:Coenagrionidae) -a wandering opportunist? *Entomologists Record* **101**, 25-26

Fox, A.D. & Cham, S.A. (1994) Status, Habitat use and conservation of the Scarce Blue-tailed Damselfly *Ischnura pumilio* (Charpentier) In Britain and Ireland. Biological Conservation **68**, 115-122

Hine, R.L. (1934) *The Natural History of the Hitchin Region.* Hitchin and District Regional Survey Association.

Gladwin, T.W. (1997) A review of the species of Dragonflies (Odonata) recorded as having been observed in Hertfordshire. *Trans.Herts. Nat.Hist.Soc.* 33 (1), 56-61.

Hodgson, S.B. (1959) West Hertfordshire Dragonflies *Trans. Herts. Nat. Hist. Soc.* **25,** 68-72.

Ketelaar, R. (2000) European reports 1999: The Netherlands, Odonata. *Atropos* **10**, 47-49

Lloyd, B. (1937) Dragonflies at Elstree Reservoir and District. *Transactions HNHS* **20**, 89-90

Lloyd, B. (1944) West Hertfordshire Dragonflies *Transactions HNHS* **22**, 43-47

Lloyd, S. (1948). Report on Dragonflies observed in Hertfordshire in 1946. *Transactions HNHS* **23**, 21-23.

Lloyd, S. (1953) Report on Dragonflies observed in Hertfordshire in 1950-1951. *Transactions HNHS* **24**, 35-37.

Longfield, C. (1937) *The Dragonflies of the British Isles.* Warne, London.

Lucas, W.J. (1900) *British Dragonflies (Odonata).* Upcott Gill, London.

Mendel, H. (1992) *Suffolk Dragonflies* Suffolk Naturalist' Society, Ipswich

Merritt, R., Moore, N.W. and Eversham, B.C. (1996) *Atlas of the Dragonflies of Britain and Ireland.* HMSO London

Milne, B.S. (1984) The dragonfly fauna of the Ouse Valley gravel pits. *J.Br.Dragonfly Soc.* **1** (4), 55-59.

Moore, N.W. (1997) *Dragonflies - Status Survey and Conservation Action Plan.* IUCN, Gland, Switzerland and Cambridge.

Moore, N.W. (2002) *Oaks, Dragonflies and People - Creating a small nature reserve and relating its story to wider conservation issues.* Harley Books, Colchester, Essex.

Nau, B.S., Boon, C.R. and Knowles, J.P. (1987). *Bedfordshire Wildlife.* Castlemead Publications, Ware.

Palmer, R. (1930) Dragonflies observed in Hertfordshire. *Trans. Herts. Nat. Hist. Soc,* **19**, 48-50.

Palmer, R. (1940) Hertfordshire Dragonflies. *Trans. Herts. Nat. Hist. Soc,* **21**, 167-172

Palmer, R. (1947) Bedfordshire Dragonflies. *Bedfordshire Naturalist.* **2**, 30-33.

Palmer, R. (1949) Report on Odonata (for 1948). *Bedfordshire Naturalist.* **3,** 26-27

Palmer, R. (1949) The Reptiles and Amphibians of Bedfordshire. *Bedfordshire Naturalist.* **4**, 36-39.

Palmer, R. (1950) Unusual accident to a dragonfly. *Bedfordshire Naturalist.* **5**, 47

Palmer, R. (1951) Report for Odonata (for 1950). *Bedfordshire Naturalist.* **5**

Palmer, R. (1943-1952) extracts from Index of Odonata (personal record cards).

Prince, P. and Clarke, C. (1993) The Hobby's breeding range in Britain. What factors have allowed it to expand? *British Wildlife* 4 (6), 341-346.

Reid, D.A. (1951) Dragonflies. In notes and observations. *Bedfordshire Naturalist.* **6**, 35.

Revels, R. (2000) *Wild Bedfordshire.* The Bedfordshire Natural History Society

Rich, T. (1998) Squaring the circles *British Wildlife* **9**, 213-219

Smallshire, D. and Swash, A. (2004) *Britain's Dragonflies.* WILDguides, Old Basing

Speyer, E.R. (1949) An occurrence of *Ischnura pumilio* Charp. (Odonata) in Hertfordshire. *Jnl.Soc. for Brit. Ent.* **3**, 45

Stephens, J.F. (1836) *Illustrations of British Entomology.* Vol **6**.

Thompson, D. (1997) *The 'Azure Damselfly' in Brooks, S. (1997) Field Guide to the Dragonflies and Damselflies of Great Britain and Ireland.* British Wildlife Publishing.

Verdcourt, B. (1945) Records of Odonata-Zygoptera from Bedfordshire. *Ent.Mon.Mag.* **81**, 75

Verdcourt, B. (1986) Some Early Dragonfly Records from Bedfordshire. *Muntjac; (newsletter of the B.N.H.S.)* **62**, 4

Wasscher, M. (1999) Identification of Small Red-eyed Damselfly *Erythromma viridulum* (Charp.) *Atropos* 7, 7-9.

West, B.B. (1975) Annual report of Felmersham NR. *Ardea* **25** November 1975, 6-7

West, K.E. (1953) Odonata - Report of the recorder (for 1952). *Bedfordshire Naturalist.* 7, 24

West, K.E. (1959) Odonata - Report of the recorder (for 1957). *Bedfordshire Naturalist.* **12**, 30

West, K.E. (1959) Odonata - Report of the recorder (for 1958). *Bedfordshire Naturalist.* **13**, 33-35

West, K.E. (1960) Odonata - Report of the recorder (for 1959). *Bedfordshire Naturalist.* **14**, 43-44

Williams, P., Biggs, J., Corfield, A., Fox, G., Walker, D. & Whitfield, M. (1997) Designing New Ponds for Wildlife. *British Wildlife* 8 (3), 137-150.

Winsland, D.C. (1983) Some observations of *Erythromma najas* (Hansemann) *J.Br.Dragonfly Soc.* **1**, 6

Species index

Place index